What It Takes

The inspiring insight of a boys football journey from childhood dreams to professional footballer

Aaron Tighe

This book is dedicated to

Julie, my true soul mate, and Sean and Megan, may you experience all the wonders of life, Love Dad.

To all those players who have shared the sweat, tears, and joy of a professional footballers life, be it for a short time or long. Congratulations on your amazing achievements.

Mum, Dad, Graham and Derek. A better family you couldn't wish for.

" Time goes by in a rush of no mercy, like a river of night and day"

— Aaron Tighe, "Please stay a while" Copyright©
1991

*" The day will come of this I'm sure, I'll drag myself up off the floor,
be the man I want to be, take my chances, and succeed. Convince me
that my hope is good, convince me cause I know it should, deliver
me from all I've done, all I've lost and all I've won"*

— Aaron Tighe, "where the thundering dies"
Copyright© 1991

*" It is not the critic who counts, nor the man who points out how
the strong man stumbles or where the doer of deeds could have done
better. The credit belongs to the man who is actually in the arena,
whose face is marred by dust and sweat and blood: who knows
great enthusiasm, great devotion and the triumph of achievement
and who, at the worst, if he fails, at least fails while doing greatly –
so that his place shall never be with those cold and timid souls who
know neither victory nor defeat......"*

— Theodore Roosevelt, "Citizen in a Republic"
23rd April 1910

Contents

Introduction

THE INSPIRATION

I was fortunate enough today to be a member of a business-orientated audience who had gathered to listen to two of the world's leading sales and marketing gurus Zig Ziglar and Jim Rohn. I was pleasantly surprised to find that these immensely successful people were to offer philosophies and advice on not business alone but also how to succeed in this thing called life.

Zig Ziglar with his slow American drawl, is, as I write, over seventy years old with the energy of a nine-year-old and the wisdom of a very successful man. One of his many stories today was how he had written his first book as a young poor man by simply writing one page and one-fourth per day for one year. His story was to prove that amazing things can happen from small steps, as long as you know where you're going and how you're going to get there.

I thought "Hey, I could do that" and so here I am writing my football tale. This is day one and if you're reading this then you know that I was successful in my pursuit. I hope you enjoy my memories, they are precious to me. Some are fantastic, some are exciting, some are funny and some bring back a lot of pain. One thing is for sure, they have made me what I am. This is my football story.

Prologue

"I'm fit John, can I go?" I asked, silently praying that my coach's answer would set me on my way to fulfill my dream of representing my country in an international football match. This despite the fact that I had not played or trained for over three weeks due to ankle ligament damage caused by the amazing feat of jumping over a sack of balls in the narrow corridor off the player's tunnel whereby I managed to absently underestimate the required jumping distance, rolling my landing foot off the top of an unseen ball. I had just successfully come through a grueling indoor, hard wooden floor, five-a-side tournament to prove my fitness levels, strapping my badly damaged ankle so tight that I had to put on an extra boot size just to get the thing on, this being the only way to push the through the debilitating pain threshold.

This was absolutely necessary as I had been informed the previous day that I had been asked to represent my country but my club had properly declined, informing the international officials that I was currently injured and could not travel. Although this was fact and true, they hadn't taken into account the determination and desperation of this young player to represent his country at the international level and somehow I had convinced my coach to give me the opportunity to prove my fitness the next day at the 5 a side tournament, signaling to the International officials to hold the place for 24 hours.

The challenge for me as I ran out with the team to compete on the hard surface was not only to get on the ball and play well but also to show no signs of flinching in tackles, limping on turns, or general signs of pain or else the coach John would say a big final no to my international adventure. Physically I had strapped the ankle so tight it could not move and now mentally I had to forget the sharp, shooting pains endured every time I placed my body weight onto the stressed ankle ligaments.

Within minutes a couple of well-timed tackles and a dismissing of the concentrated pain boosted my fragile confidence and with a glance over at our determined but unmoved coach I knew I could get through the tournament games intact. As my confidence grew so did my ability to influence the games with my playmaker approach and before we knew it, the tournament was in the bag and we had cruised through to win the final.

So here I was in the dressing room alone with the coach post the final, post the celebrations of victory, and post my "question I'm fit John can I go?" It was one of those moments where time stands still as you await your fate. John hesitated, looked away, I waited, and then hunting down the truth, he looked me straight in the eye and asked "Are you sure you feel fit?" "Yes I feel great John" I replied hiding the fact that the pain was only just bearable. Still staring me out John nodded." Well you looked okay to me, you can go" "Yesssssssssss!" I said with a grin from ear to ear.

The fate of a footballer walks the tightrope of such moments. Not only did I play in the international match but I also led out my country as captain, how close I was to missing that opportunity. God how I loved football at that moment!

THE GREEN AND EARLY BEGINNINGS

Aaron Patrick Tighe was born at 3 pm on the afternoon of the eleventh day of July 1969 at the Horton Hospital in Banbury, Oxfordshire, England. Man was just about to land on the moon and it was the summer of love in America. I was Mum's third child and third boy and was named after a jumper that my Mum was knitting at the time called an Aran. The nurse later told Mum and Dad that the pronunciation was actually Airun and that was that. We now had a family of five; Mum, Dad, baby Aaron, and my two brothers Graham and Derek aged 6 and 5.

We lived at the time in Bretch Hill, a Banbury council estate with red-brick terraced houses in typical English style. Our house was at the end of a terrace that faced out onto a small park. Houses, low front garden bushes, and a narrow concrete footpath surrounded the "Green" as we called it on three sides, with Bretch Hill Road acting as the enclosing boundary.

Mum and Dad had spent most of their adult life in England having traveled over from Dublin to find work and a new life for themselves. Mum came from a family of five sisters; my Mum Rose Marie, Patsie, Sylvia, Ettna, and Bernie. Amazingly in a time when the youth of Ireland emigrated on a large scale, she was the only member of her family to do so. Mum's Mum, May Casey, otherwise known as Grannie to us kids, was a wonderful woman who had remarried after the death of my Mum's father Patrick Doyle at the early age of 40. Grannie's new husband Tom Casey was a fantastic Grandad to us kids and possessed a zest for life that matched his stature as a big man. It was always a warm feeling to be around them

My Dad also came from a strong Dublin family, made up of five brothers. There was my Dad Andrew Leo, Ray, Jim, Des, Noel, and solitary sister Doreen. Unlike the Doyle's/Casey's, virtually all of Dad's clan ventured to other countries to seek a new life. My Dad's parents Maureen and Charlie Tighe, otherwise fondly known as Nanna and Grandad remained in Captains Road Crumlin, a well-known suburb of Dublin. Visiting their home was like coming home ourselves, with Nanna's massive big hug and Grandad's famous magic tricks and entertainment. Grandad told me that his father had been on the stage in Dublin and was a real entertainer. He obviously followed suit. Even into his late 80's he had people rolling in the aisles at parties and social gatherings. Great people!

Mum and Dad, after trying various English towns eventually settled in Banbury and worked hard to provide us kids with a good home; Dad working in the local car factory at Cowley and Mum waitressing in the town. Dad had previously been in the RAF for three years and had spent time overseas in Germany and Europe. He was a tough dedicated man and a father who spent all of his time with his family and wasn't one for following the other men down the pub, a good attribute that I would always follow. Mum despite working as well, was always there when we needed her and had a great knack for washing us in the sink so we could still watch our buddies playing out on the 'Green'.

Now I must explain that in my memory as a small boy, the "Green" was the size of a football pitch with an even playing surface and beautiful lush green grass. It was our Wembley Stadium, Old

Trafford, Anfield, Goodison Park, and White Hart Lane all rolled into one. Of course in reality that was not quite the truth and the "Green" was in fact a bumpy, patchy, area of grass with holes everywhere that you could drown in when they were filled with water. However, for my memory's sake let's think of it as Wembley.

Imaginary cup finals and internationals were played and fought out here amongst the young boys who lived in the vicinity. The winners would do laps of honour waving into the houses surrounding, the Mums peering out the kitchen windows and waving back. I can remember how in awe I was when I saw one of the older boys take a throw in one day. The ball went from one side of the "Green" to the other in a looping motion. To a four or five-year-old like me, it was an amazing feat. Can you imagine someone doing that at Wembley! Our "Green" was a place where heroes were carried aloft on shoulders and the losers; well there was always tomorrow's game.

Our back garden was also a place where many football skills were learned during my early years. At the back of our house, my Dad had laid a concrete drive with two big blue gates as the entrance out onto the road. I would spend endless hours kicking my ball against these blue gates pretending I was Martin Dobson from Everton. My brother Graham encouraged me to kick with my left foot, which then became my favoured foot and both Graham and Derek also set out to teach me how to head the ball. Graham was about 11 at this time and here he was throwing the ball to me a five-year-old saying "time it, time it" as it bounced off my nose or the crown of my head. I mean what does 'time it' mean to a five-year-old? These lessons at an early age must have been of great benefit to me and I would encourage similar basic practices for all youngsters. The thing is once you start kicking a ball around it's a great feeling and from that, the interest grows.

Now for some reason as a youngster, I supported Everton Football Club. I think it was purely down to the fact that the first soccer-playing card that I possessed featured an Everton player, the aforementioned Martin Dobson. From that moment on he became my hero, much to the amazement of my family who were Man United and Arsenal supporters. At the time soccer playing cards were an important facet of life at St Joseph's, my junior school. My mates Martin Whitman, Jimmy Minchin, and I all regularly had competitions to attempt to win more cards from each other. These cards were a valuable status symbol in the classroom, so collecting more and more took dedicated work from us 6 and 7-year-olds. Winning them from each other became the major way to increase your collection, as buying them from the shops was not always an option if your parents were on a tight budget.

To win we would simply stand five or ten yards away from a wall and flick our card towards the wall. The nearest to the wall won and he would then get to keep the other cards that had been played. Learning to flick your card in a particular way became a real art and the competition was hot. I ended up with tins full of cards and kept them for many years. I think my folks gave them away in one of their many house moves. Ah well, farewell, Martin Dobson!

The back garden was also the scene for my first football injury around this time. Martin Whitman who lived opposite us on the Green had come over for a kickabout. My Mum and Dad weren't about and my brother Graham was left looking after us. With Graham in the house at the time, me and Martin were kicking the ball to each other in the back when I accidentally kicked the ball over the fence into the next-door neighbour's garden. The fence was quite a low one but big to a little one like me and was made of a green wire crisscrossed in a net effect. The ends of the wire at the top of the fence were barbed wire-like and pretty sharp. Every five yards or so there were steel rods stuck into the ground supporting the fence. We would place a bit of wood on top of these and use the wood as a step to get over the fence. I quickly climbed over the fence, retrieved the ball, and threw it to Martin in our garden. As I did, I heard footsteps in the passage leading to our neighbour's garden. Fearing that he may catch me in ' his' garden and do some dreadful thing to me, I ran towards the fence for a quick undetected escape.

As I got my foot on the top of the fence and my weight transferred to that foot, I slipped catching the back of my knee on one of the spiky wires protruding from the top. The momentum downwards meant that my leg followed leaving my skin at the top of the fence. The screams would have awoken the dead and before I knew it Graham and our neighbour were carrying me inside and mopping up the blood that was pouring down my leg. Graham was saying things like " Ahh I can see the bones" which didn't help to take my mind off the pain! Later, Dad arrived home, took a look at my leg, and said calmly and almost proudly "come on son we're going down the hospital for some stitches" I replied with "ahh it's not that bad Dad". But the stitches went in and my first scar appeared.

The Primrose family were best friends with us Tighe's and lived at the other end of the Green. The lovely Madeleine Primrose, the Mum of the household often looked after me while my Mum was at work. James and David, her two sons, were a bit older than me but that didn't stop us being good mates. David and I in particular got on famously. Jam es was an Arsenal supporter through and through whilst David followed ' the Spurs'.

David and I would play a game called ' goalie to goalie' on the Green for hours on end. In fact entire tournaments would sometimes be held. Let me explain how the game worked. A tree with a coat or jumper 6/7 yards away would be one goal, whilst directly opposite a similar goal was set up. We would stand opposite each other and take turns shooting and saving. The first to reach 10 goals was the winner and a competitive frenzy would commence between us.

On one occasion a pressure shot had arrived in one of our Cup finals. We were locked at 9v9 and it was my turn to shoot. I only had to score to win. This was going to be my best shot I thought to myself. I placed the ball down, took a few steps back, and then with my left foot struck the sweetest shot of my young footballing life. The ball glided through the air as if in slow motion towards the top left-hand corner of the goal.

Now people claim that Gordon Banks made the greatest ever save in football history. During a World Cup match between England and Brazil in 1970, he flicked a powerful Pele header up over the bar from his bottom right-hand corner. Although a magnificent save it ranked second to what was about to happen on "The Green" Banbury England 1975 ish, from the middle of his goal David Primrose launched himself skyward towards his top right-hand corner and with his outstretched right hand flicked the ball around the tree, sorry, post to safety. It was a monumental moment and whoever won the final after that didn't matter; all we talked about for days was 'the save'!

As well as on the Green and in my back garden my early school days were also filled with plenty of football activity. Martin W hitman my best mate was a year younger than me which meant that during playtime in the playground, he was not allowed to play with us as the older kids were separated from the younger ones by a dividing basketball line on the tarmac ground. Football however crosses all boundaries. I would stand on one side of the line whilst Martin stood on the other and we'd kick a football back and forth across the line to each other. If we didn't have a football we'd use anything that could be kicked, such as bits of ice in the winter or those little bouncy rubber balls which were great fun and hard to control.

By the age of seven, I had developed ball skills that were above average and was now receiving the respect of my fellow footballing peers. One summer it was decided that a five-a-side football tournament would be held at school, during the hour-long lunch break. St Josephs School had plenty of grass for us to set up two pitches and immediately we set to work on selecting our teams.

I recruited my own team, naming us the 'Tigers', probably due to the fact that it was similar to my own name and that I had a red and white T-shirt with Tigers emblasoned across the front. The lads I recruited were most of my own close mates who were the same age or younger, which meant we would be up against older teams, but we didn't care as we set out on the road to glory. This was my first true experience of teamwork and it was filled with the highs and lows, which were to be experienced so often later in life.

We fought and died for each other during the games, eventually reaching the final after disposing of a few older teams along the way. The final was the real test as a team called 'The Reds' stood between victory and us. James Primrose from down the green captained the Reds and had recruited the best players with transfer fees of bars of chocolate and playing cards. It was to be my first bitter taste of defeat. Although we battled hard, they were too good for us and ran away with the game. James Primrose paraded the cup, a miniature European champions cup from Subbuteo, around the pitch as me and the lads treaded off, heads down back to class.

At this time my football ability was also recognised by the local Cub Scouts (years later my ability would be recognised by a different type of scout) and I was signed up to my first eleven-a-side football team, with proper orange football shirts and all the gear. My Mum would come down to watch me play on the weekend even though she didn't have a clue about the rules, God love her. It was a good bunch of kids having lots of fun and at the end of the season, I was awarded with a player of the season award, a plaque that I still treasure to this day.

Sadly the era of 'the Green', my early football learning ground drew to a close during late 1976. My parents had decided to buy their first home, which meant that we had to move out of the area. What was a young boy to do?

One day at my new home in Morris Drive Banbury the pull of my friends and the need for a good old game of football got the better of me and I decided without asking permission to visit my old mates on the Green. I set off on my bike ride totally oblivious to danger, crossing fields, major roads and God knows what else, reaching the Green safely and in one piece. Of course, a great game of football was had and then the arduous journey back home began. When I eventually got home I found my poor Mum waiting anxiously for her 7-year-old wondering where the hell I'd been. It was to be my last game of football on the Green, the end of an era.

BANBURY AND MANCHESTER UNITED

The Primrose family was fortunately also big supporters of the local non-league football team Banbury United. As I was now seven or eight years old I was allowed to join them in attending Banbury Utd's home games, where I'd stand on the terraces with my mates James and David. It was here from behind the goal that I began to learn the wonderful chants of football supporters, some crude and some just plain good old fun. Banbury at the time had a terrific center-forward called Oliie Kearns who later went on to have a successful professional career with Reading. Whenever he got around the ball we'd join in with "Ollie Ollie Ollie, oy, oy, oy" and this song was surpassed by my favourite whenever our winger Steve Slaughter got on the ball. To the tune of the Christmas carol 'Deck the Halls' you'd hear us at the top of our voices singing "Stevie Slaughter walks on water la la la la - la la la la la." In a twist of fate the song "Deck the Halls" would be performed by me in its true format some years later in a manner that I will never forget but more of that later. It's funny the things that stick in your memory as a kid as I can't remember anything about the games that took place on those Saturday afternoons at Banbury but do recall standing once in a packed crowd behind one of the goals when after an exciting moment in the game the crowd swooped forward in a big push and I was crushed at the front by the barriers, a very frightening moment for a little one like me. That was the last time I stood on the terraces and opted for the safety of the main stand from then on.

My first visit to a professional football match would have been around 1976 and what a team to take me to see. My Dad took me along to Birmingham City versus Manchester United at St Andrews Birmingham. This was the Tommy Docherty era at Man Utd. The team was an exciting attacking team with players like Gordon Hill, Gerry Daly, and Steve Coppell. I can remember Gerry Daly scoring a penalty and being thrilled by the noise and the atmosphere surrounding the game. Little did I know at the time that many years later I would receive a phone call from a certain Gerry Daly asking me if I wanted to join his team!

From that moment on Everton was ditched and I was welcomed by my uncles and Dad into the Tighe's Man United fan club. Around this time I also paid my first visit to the amazing Old Trafford, the home of Man Utd. My Dad accompanied me along with my uncles Des and Noel, who were over from Ireland visiting. All of my uncles were and still are fanatical followers of the game and in particular Man U. Uncle Des was always heavily involved in the Dublin amateur scene and later in the semi-professional scene with Dublin side St Patrick's Athletic (where the great Paul Mc Grath of Ireland and Manchester United was discovered). Although my Dad never played football seriously, he would sometimes tell stories about how he and his brothers played football out in the back garden of my Nana's house in Crumlin Dublin. I'd say he must have played quite a bit as even now Dad has a pretty good touch on the ball. Maybe he should have taken it up seriously, who knows what might have happened.

On this particular visit to Old Trafford we encountered a pretty big hitch, the match was sold out and we didn't have any tickets, a potential disaster for a carload of Man Utd fanatics who had traveled across from Ireland to see the game. As it happened though, a miracle occurred, as a kind-hearted gentleman whose son couldn't make the game gave us his spare ticket. Apparently, he had seen me and my Dad looking despondent by the turnstiles and amazingly gave us the ticket. We were in! Dad lifted me over the turnstiles and we went. Poor Des and Noel had to resort to listening to the game on the radio in their car, not ideal but a least they could say they had gone to Old Trafford! The atmosphere inside the ground was electric. I think the game was also against Birmingham and although I can't remember what went on in the game I do recall being amazed by the size of the place and being blown away by it all. From that moment on I dreamed of playing for the great Manchester United. After the game on the way home, just to add to my uncle's woes we managed to run out of petrol on the motorway and I have a lasting memory of my Uncle Noel dashing across fields in search of a petrol station so we could get home. Poor Dad was fuming that no one had noticed the petrol gauge including himself. I didn't really care though, as I was lost still thinking about the amazing event that I had just witnessed and was now dreaming of playing football with my heroes.

DUBLIN IRELAND

1977 - 1984

A gigantic change was to occur in my life in late 1977. My parents had decided to head back across the water to Dublin. I was eight at the time and didn't really understand what was happening but knew things were going to be a lot different. Banbury had been a good place for me. Close friendships with boys I had grown up with during my eight short years had been forged and I was settled into St Joseph's school but change it must.

Before we left my Dad arranged for me to receive the next best thing to meet the Manchester United players and that was to meet the Banbury United team. It was to be one of the highlights of my young life. I met the players in the dressing room before the match between Banbury and Bromsgrove, managing to get all of their autographs in a little yellow autograph book that was treasured for years to come. I also had the privilege of running out onto the pitch with them, joining in the warm-up, and playing football on the hallowed turf of the Banbury Utd pitch. A photo was taken with the team with me dead centre and so it came about that my early Banbury years had drawn to a memorable close.

Aaron Tighe

As an adult I returned to visit Banbury and 'the Green', to see the place where I had learned my early football skills and was sadly amazed to see the grassed park that we once imagined to be Wembley, littered with parked cars. The boyhood memory was unfortunately now a scruffy bit of unkept old ground. As my Mum said, "That would never have happened in our day." However, I will always remember it as I saw it when I was four, five, six, and seven, a magical place where I learned the beautiful game that would take over my life.

We arrived in Dublin during November 1977. Mum and Dad put us three kids on the plane, a luxury at the time. We were picked up and looked after by relatives whilst Mum and Dad followed on the car ferry with all of our possessions. Graham the eldest was 14 at the time, Derek was 13 and little Aaron was 8 years old. Thinking back now it must have been a tough time for us kids and particularly my brothers who were leaving settled surroundings for a completely new country and Ireland at that. Being and sounding English in Dublin wasn't a problem for a little kid like me but for my brothers, I dare say they may have taken a little bit of stick from the other kids upon hearing the accent.

The first four months were spent at my Grannies house in Rathfarnham. Granny, shooie (a beautiful little Pomeranian dog), and my Grandad Tom were great folks and offered Mum and Dad a place to stay whilst they hunted around for a house. Rathfarnham is one of the many suburbs located south of the river in Dublin and had a completely different look and feel to Banbury. Grannies house was a 3 bedroom terraced house with small gardens front and rear and always a homely atmosphere attached. Despite this, I quickly found that I really missed my friends in Banbury and would cry myself to sleep at night. from being a popular kid on the block with many mates to play football with, I now knew no one and found it extremely difficult to adjust. I would play imaginary games of football in the living room using a cushion as a ball, doing the commentary and crowd noises all in one breath. Being winter the weather would have been pretty bad hence the reason for indoor entertainment. However, nothing could take my mind off my friends and how I longed for Banbury!

Eventually Mum and Dad found a house that they liked in Old Bawn Tallaght. Tallaght was originally a little village southwest of Dublin known for its history as a mass grave during the Irish famine in the 19th century and in more modern times its pub 'Bridget Burkes'. Old Bawn was a new estate within what was now a densely populated urban prawl, overlooked by the Wicklow Mountains with the famous Hell Fire club ruins at their summit. I was enrolled at the local Scoil Maelruan which was a two-minute walk from our house whilst Graham and Derek had to travel by bike to the older Tallaght community school, about 5 miles away. Old Bawn being new was fortunately for me, full of young families, which meant plenty of boys keen to play football. With my football skills already well developed I soon became a popular kid at school and made a few friends, which helped greatly in settling me down into my new surroundings.

A few of the guys in my class played football for the local team Tymon Bawn and Alan Jordan the leader of the gang asked if I wanted to come to training. Without hesitation I accepted and before I knew it I was enlisted to play for Tymon Bawn under 10's, along with my friends Eddi e Meade, Mark Pollock (fluky), Keith Tighe (Tighser - my cousin), Mark Sherlock, and Paddy Kiernan. If I can remember rightly we used to train one evening a week in the school hall and then play on the weekends, paying our 50 pence subs (subscriptions) weekly to make sure we got a game. In those days there were no such things as changing rooms and we would arrive for the game with our shorts and socks on, find the biggest tree to hide from the freezing wind, sleet, rain, or snow, whip off our coats, jumpers, shirts, and vests and quickly pull the football shirt over our heads and run as fast as we could towards the pitch to warm up. If any of the lads happened to wear a vest under their shirt they were berated and considered a cissy despite the freezing conditions. The beautiful thing about those situations was that we knew no different and everyone just got on with it. The conditions helped to foster camaraderie and it was all considered part of the fun.

My ability as a budding center-forward was quickly recognised by the managers Noel Cummins and Paul Holohan and for a number of years running I was nominated player of the year and top goalscorer. Noel told me years later that I had the ability to use both feet and a natural control of the ball and that was what made me stand out on the pitch. I once heard the great Bobby Charlton say that the thing a scout looks for is balance and easy control and movement of the ball. Any kid that wants to be a player needs to capture that skill and the only way is to practice with the ball as much as possible.

UNITED HERE WE COME

It was around this time that my Dad began to get involved in football and helped out with the management of our team. I think he recognised that I showed some potential and wanted to support that in the best way that he could. He and Paul Holohan, our manager, arranged a couple of trips to England for the team at the end of the season. Games were arranged against local teams and more importantly, tickets to watch our hero's Manchester United play. The first time we went, we stayed at a local YMCA in Manchester and had a great laugh. For a bunch of Dublin kids, it was a great experience to be away from home all huddled together in this strange place. I remember the YMCA had a large indoor swimming pool with far too much chlorine in it, which took its toll on one of our players David Lawlor. Poor David was suffering badly with his eyes after keeping them open whilst swimming underwater in the pool. David was literally blinded to the great amusement of the rest of the lads. To add to the fun, at lunch the lads put all sorts of stuff in David's drink without him being able to see what was going on. He'd take a sip and spit it out rapidly to great roars of laughter from his teammates, poor old David.

Although David's misfortune still sticks in my memory the highlight of the trip was the Manchester United match. The fixture was Man Utd v. Liverpool in a top-of-the-table clash. United won 2 - 1 in front of 58,000 people and the atmosphere was sensational. None of us could speak the next day, the result of shouting and screaming at the top of our lungs. Although not quite as euphoric as the Man U game we also went along to see Manchester City play at their home ground Maine Road. I can recall us precariously leaning over the advertising hoarding that surrounds the pitch grabbing blades of grass to take home as mementos of the occasion. We were seated directly behind Man City's goal where their well-known goalie Joe Corrigan stood. Before the game, Joe handed a rose to an elderly woman in the crowd who during the game continually stood up and rang a big school-like bell when she got excited, deafening all around her. She tended to get excited quite often so God help the season ticket holders who had to put up with that every week! Saying that It was all done in good fun and whenever I watched City play on television for years later you would always hear that bell ringing in the background, an amazing lady, and amazingly for me the next time I'd return to Maine Road was as a player with Luton Town but more of that later.

For a kid like me who was a football fanatic, I can't state too much how important events like these were in my life. The footballers that we saw at these games were icons, heroes, and the biggest stars imaginable. We all dreamed of being a professional footballer and when I say dreamed it would be comparable to a kid dreaming of flying to the moon. It was the same scope of dream, something, which was like gold at the end of the rainbow, imaginable but a million miles away from reality.

During this trip to England, it was arranged for us to visit Manchester United's ground Old Trafford for a tour of the facilities. We were all extremely excited by this and had visions of getting the ball out on the pitch for a kickabout. Unfortunately, it wasn't that type of tour but we did get to see all of the conference and function rooms! Actually, some of our team members did leave the ground that day with souvenirs of a cutlery nature with the Manchester United logo as proof of where they came from. Say no more! The best part of the tour though was viewing the pitch from high up in the stand and what followed. As the tour party made its way back inside the stand my Dad held me back and then guided me down towards the pitch meandering in and out of the seats and terracing until finally we were down beside the pitch. When we were sure no one was looking we crept out onto the pitch and I stood in the goal at the Stretford end in total awe at what surrounded me. I felt like a gladiator in a Roman arena and imagined 60,000 supporters chanting and bustling around the ground. It was a magic moment and I sucked in the air as if to make me realise 'this is real'. This was little Aaron Tighe from Old Bawn Dublin standing in the goal at Old Trafford the home of my heroes, truly amazing stuff. Later we visited the souvenir shop and whilst queuing caught site of one of the players Mickey Thomas. He was gone before we could ask him for an autograph but it was a real buzz to be close to one of our heroes.

As the weekend trip drew to a close we were all in great spirits as we made our way back home to Dublin on the Sealink ferry and couldn't wait to get home to tell all our friends and family about the amazing experience we had been through. As we hung on dearly to the ship railings up on deck due to rough seas, we sang songs together, a great Irish tradition, until one by one our singing unfortunately turned to throwing up over the side. Dad was the ringleader for the singing shouting, "Keep singing lads it will take your mind off it!"

These were good times in my life, apart from school, which was just too boring for me. I'd literally sit in class willing the minute hand to go faster. In a short time, I had settled in well in my new home and surroundings. I was a popular kid with lots of good friends, playing football whenever and wherever I could. What more could a young boy want? Although I had won some personal awards for playing football the time had come for our team to be rewarded for our efforts also. We were in division 12H which I suppose stood for Under 12's division 8. That doesn't sound too good but Dublin at the time had the biggest schoolboy football league in Europe and in the under-12 section we were in one of the middle leagues which shows the scale of the amount of teams competing. Everything had excitedly come down to the last game of the season to decide the fate of the championship and we faced our challenger Neilstown Rangers. Whoever won the game won the championship and would be promoted the following season. Victory on the day was ours due to a cracking goal by our big gangly center-forward and good friend Mark Pollock AKA Fluky. The celebrations when the final whistle went were ecstatic. Fluky with his bobble hat on his head, and shirtsleeves stretched halfway up his arm, because he was too big for them, ran towards me with his gangly arms and legs flailing everywhere. We embraced and jumped for joy, the League was ours and all the hard work had paid off. A celebratory dinner ensued at a local restaurant and we began to plan for the next season, which was sure to be a lot tougher. The victory promoted us to division 13D a big jump of 4 divisions and a big challenge for our dedicated local community team.

SPORTSMAN OF THE YEAR
1981

Football was not the only sport I was involved in during these years. My school had recognised an overall sporting ability in me and I represented them in Basketball, Gaelic football, and Athletics. I was a big fan of basketball in my 5th and 6th year of primary school and although not the tallest of kids had good dribbling abilities and half-decent shooting skills. I ended up with some other kids from various schools being selected to represent the community schools of Ireland in a basketball exhibition match, which was apparently video'd and sent to all schools to be used as an example of how basketball should be played. It was a funny experience as we had to do lots of training for this one game and there was a real build-up to this event. We played the game in front of a stand full of screaming kids at an indoor arena and then we never heard any more. I never even got to see the televised event! Looking back it would have been great to see but basketball was just one of a number of sports that were going on at the time and I didn't have time to think "Oh what happened to that televised footage" which was a pity as I'm sure it would have been good to look back on.

Aaron Tighe

Athletics was the other main sport that I was involved in at school and two disciplines in particular, Long distance and hurdling. I can honestly say that I never enjoyed athletics, particularly long-distance. I think the reason was that although I was the best in my school at these events I was nowhere near the best amongst Dublin's selected athletes. In fact thinking back I just could never see where the enjoyment came from unless you were winning. I mean football was so different. There are so many different facets to the game. You get enjoyment from scoring a goal, making a great pass, tackling, shooting, being part of a team etc etc. Don't get me wrong, I'm not saying people shouldn't do athletics; it's just that it didn't do anything for me. As a professional footballer, I would use long distances as a measurement of my fitness and a way to get fit. It's terrific for stamina building. However, I could never say it was enjoyable.

All of this sporting activity was to pay off in my final year at Scoil Maelruan. At the end of every school year, the teachers would announce various awards for achievement. The awards ceremony was held in the sports hall and culminated with the announcement of sportsman and woman of the year. On this occasion, the hall was packed with kids and teachers and one by one the various awards were given out by the headmaster Mr. Rafferty, a big man who scared the hell out of all of us. Sportswoman of the Year was announced first and classmate Audrey Nicholson was the winner, a popular decision as the kids clapped and cheered. That left the final award 'sportsman of the Year' to be announced. I knew that I was in the running for the prize but was up against some stiff opposition. A guy by the name of John Cullen was one of Irelands' top 100-metre sprinters and had won various big races throughout the year. The tension built as Mr. Rafferty stepped up to the mic. "And Sportsman of the Year for 1980/81 goes to" At this kind of moment in a split second, I find your mind prepares yourself for defeat, but also throws forward an expectancy to win. Either way, these are special moments. "Aaron Tighe" As my name was spoken a rush of joy swept over me and before I knew it I was up receiving my award in front of the entire school. All of my peers, competitors, and friends were clapping and cheering. My classmates then set to carrying me aloft on their shoulders back to our classroom. I was one of them and we had won. What a way to finish your time at a school. I shall never forget it, a truly wonderful moment in my young life.

THE CORNER, WALL and
SIGN POST

Where we lived in Old Bawn Tallaght, the houses were all the same style; 3-bedroom semi-detached two-story homes with an attached garage on the side. The houses had a pebbledash finish over the brickwork at the bottom and the second floors were generally painted a creamy colour up to the roof. The gardens were small front and back with low concrete block walls surrounding them. We were situated facing the entry to a close by the name of Watermead close. The roads in Old Bawn were concrete with strips of tar cris crossing the road where sections of concrete met. This gave us tennis-like courts to play all sorts of games on, such as actual tennis and more importantly football tennis. Football tennis had the same rules as normal tennis, the only differences being you had to use your feet instead of a racquet and the ball was a lot bigger! Games of doubles and singles were not uncommon and competition was taken seriously. However, although football and tennis were great the best game that we played was called Combo, which is short for combination. On the corner of the entry to Watermeade Close was a small grass verge and situated on this verge was a big wooden sign showing the name of the road. This sign was used as our goal and the reason for it was due to its shape. It was about four feet high and wide and was made of one large block of white painted wood held by two thick white painted posts. At the bottom was a 1-foot gap, which just allowed a ball to fit through. This meant that you had a goal that didn't require a goalkeeper to make it difficult to score. Combo's rules were simple, basically to score you had to shoot the ball under the sign with a volley or a header but if you shot wide an imaginary team got a goal against you. Me and the lads Fluky, Eddie, Ajo, and gang would spend hours chipping the ball up for each other for a volley or header. The fun was being accurate with your shots because if it went wide it was a goal against. It was a great way of practicing these skills, which unknowingly we carried into our games at Tymon Bawn.

We also played a game called 'World Cup' which was a straightforward knock-out competition whereby everyone played against everyone and once you scored a goal you went through to the next round. Each of us would choose an international team to be and the last one remaining in the round was out. This would continue right through to the final where the first to score won the World Cup. Unfortunately, you didn't get to keep the trophy for four years, however, more than half an hour!

These were just a couple of games that we played on the corner as kids and like any other kids we were totally enthusiastic about winning and being the best. Our imaginations turned us into superstars until the late-night calls from our parents got us off the streets. Come rain or shine we'd throw our schoolbags inside our front doors after school and meet on the corner, or call for each other to come out and have a game of football. They were innocent days where skills and techniques were mastered through practices that were fun games, a lesson for all coaches of youngsters.

During this time on television, a 12-year-old Brazilian kid was amazing us all with his football juggling skills and tricks. The advert was for Coca-Cola and what a fantastic marketing campaign it was. They captured the attention of the entire football-mad population. I was transfixed by these skills being done by a kid who was around my age and immediately focused on copying his juggling feats. Me and the lads would hold competitions on the corner to see who could keep the ball up for the longest without using our hands. We all started off by using our good foot only but that wasn't the way the Brazilian kid did it. He used both feet alternately and could walk along comfortably whilst juggling the ball this way. I was determined to copy him and slowly but surely began to master the technique.

I started with twos and threes and before long was into the hundreds and eventually thousands. It was at this stage that I left my mates behind and finally ended up with a record of 4,411 touches of the ball before it fell to the ground. This was a pretty amazing feat as I was still only 11 years old. It just goes to show how much kids can improve through practice and determination. As I mentioned, these competitions were held on the road outside our house and we had to maneuver the ball off the road whenever a car was coming and then back onto the road once the car had gone. The Brazilian Kid did various other tricks with the ball that I practiced and practiced eventually building up a repertoire of skills that would stand me in good stead throughout my football career.

WHEN THE RAINS CAME

Ireland is a beautiful country with fantastic scenery, which rightly befits its description as 'the emerald isle'. Green it certainly is but to become such a lovely colour requires a large amount of a particular ingredient 'water'. The rain in Ireland can last for days and sometimes weeks without much of a break. It's not a downpour type but more of a drizzle that never seems to give up. It probably lends itself to the Irish culture of 'what's the hurry'. The only problem for a youngster like me was that I wanted to be outside all the time playing football and a lot of the time I found myself confined to the house with limited movement. However there was a saviour and its name was 'subbuteo' Subbuteofor those who don't know is a table football game with a cloth table size pitch, goals, 22 miniature players in a selection of playing strips, stands, scoreboards and even the Queen holding the FA Cup. Flicking your player against the ball, which imitates a kick amongst other things, plays the game. As time went by my collection grew and before long I had a whole range of teams like Man Utd, Leeds, Holland, England, Ireland etc, etc. I also had the stands with spectators, who were in turn controlled by policemen and policemen on horses. Photographers would line up behind the goals and the commentators would sit high up in the stand to have the best vantage point. I would formulate entire seasons in a copybook and play noisily on my own making all the crowd noises whilst carrying out the commentary at the same time. I think my family thought I was nuts but I simply loved the game of football and although it may have been raining outside I was still playing the game albeit in miniature! I would play my brothers on occasions but Graham in particular was a cunning opponent. The reason I say this is that during the game you would notice that you were missing a couple of players because he had taken them off the pitch while you weren't looking! We also organised a school competition one year where we all chipped in some subs (subscriptions) and I went out and bought some prizes. The prizes weren't as good as we had hoped for, as the treasurer, a lad by the name of Brendan, spent most of the money on sweets at the local shop without anyone knowing. I think he was banned from the competition and probably got a bit of stick from us lads. Subbuteo was a great game and to this day I still have most of my collection and when he's old enough, my boy will be able to play his old man at the game. I just hope he doesn't pick up his Uncles tricks!

During those rainy days, I also made a lot of use of a step in our garage. It was rare that our car was put in the garage, which adjoined our house. Although there was plenty of stuff in there, there was always enough room for me to kick the ball continuously against the step leading into the utility room. I would stand about a yard or two away and pass the ball with my left instep, then as it bounced back from the wall would control it across my body and play with the instep of my right foot. This practice taught me close control with an emphasis on setting myself up to pass the ball quickly. It meant that I developed a good touch on the ball with both feet. The tap-tap sound probably drove my family insane but I never received a word of complaint, which was great. A similar practice also took place in my garden and on the street outside our house. Our back garden was all grass with a small border around the edge. It was about 20 yards by 20 yards in size with a grey concrete block wall surrounding it, which my dad had built when we first moved in. Many hours were spent in that garden striking the ball against the wall and then controlling it as it bounced back toward me. The thud, thud sound this time must have annoyed the hall out of our neighbours but once again there were no complaints so I just kept right on doing it. The only problem with kicking a ball against a wall is that every now and again the ball goes too high, clearing the top of the wall and entering foreign airspace, landing in the neighbour's garden. When this happened you were faced with a choice, either go all the way around to your neighbours' front door, ring the doorbell, and ask for the ball back please, or alternatively, as quick as you could, scale the wall, sneak into the garden as if you were invisible, recover the football and scale the wall back to freedom. The latter was always the better option as it was quicker and a little bit scary. Saying that some walls were too high to scale and our neighbour across the street began to get annoyed with us using her wall as a battering ram and pretty soon would not return our footballs telling us in no uncertain terms to get lost when we asked for our ball back. We hated her at the time but looking back I'm not surprised she reacted the way she did we must have been a real pain.

NATIONAL SOCCER SKILLS
COMPETITION
1980

During 1980, Coca-Cola sponsored a national soccer skills tournament in Ireland. The final was to be held at Ireland's premier football ground Dalymount Park in Dublin, prior to the national cup final. Finalists would be selected from all over the country. All junior clubs were invited to send entrants to qualifying rounds within their own county and luckily for me Tymon Bawn my local club decided to send me and one of my teammates to compete.

The competition involved various events which required a variety of skills, including dribbling a ball in and out of poles without touching the poles with your body or the football, passing a ball from ten yards between two poles hitting a third which was situated behind, chipping a ball into a small circle 20 yards away, keeping the ball up etc etc. All of the events were quite difficult, so plenty of practice was required. Prior to the competition, my Dad got hold of some metal rods that we would take up to our local park and hammer into the ground. We'd lay them out exactly as in the competition and I'd practice, practice, practice, trying to perfect the techniques and skills necessary. Practice was something that came naturally to me. I was never pushed into doing it. I just simply loved kicking a ball around, In fact, I can recall running back from the local park stepping only on the grass because grass was what football was played on and I loved it because of that! You might think that this was a bit over the top but it was how fanatical I was about the game. Even now I still love the feeling of stepping out onto a lush green park with football boots on and the ball at my feet, it's a real feeling of freedom and anticipation rolled into one. It's a feeling that must be felt by people all over the world judging by the popularity of the game. These were still very innocent days when anything to do with football was fun and a good feeling. By the time the Dublin qualifiers came around, I was as near to perfection with the events as you could hope to be and was totally confident inside, which left me with little feeling of pressure. The competition went exactly according to plan and I came through with flying colours. I scored the highest score in Ireland and booked my place in the national finals. All my practicing had paid off and the feeling of being an individual winner was terrific. Leading up to the final, I practised even harder. I had got that winning feeling and didn't want to feel the other side. I wanted to be crowned the Coca-Cola soccer skills champion for Ireland and then I could compare myself to that Brazilian kid off the TV.

The final arrived and I was thrilled to be a part of it. Dalymount Park Dublin was a sell-out for the Irish equivalent of the FA Cup final and the other lads were led out onto the pitch before the game for the skills competition. It felt like we were professional footballers and the buzz of the crowd and general atmosphere was intoxicating to me. The competition started and I was led to my first event, the dribbling in and out of the poles. I was totally focused on what I had to do and knew that if I concentrated I would get maximum points comfortably. I set off with the ball at my feet closely keeping control as I weaved in and out of the poles completing the circuit relaxed, clean, and with no problems. I was elated to have completed the first event successfully and now felt totally confident that I would do well in the rest of the events. My nerves had been settled. However, as I picked up my ball to move to the next event the judge for the first event came towards me and as nice as you like said "unlucky son you touched two of the poles." As he walked away I replied shyly "I didn't touch any of the poles." My father who was watching saw that I was distressed and ran over to ask me what was wrong. On hearing what he said he dashed over to the judge had words with him and then someone else and returned with bad news. The judge would not change his decision. I was absolutely devastated, why would he say that I had touched the poles when I hadn't? I just couldn't control my anger and distress and began to choke up and cry in the middle of the football pitch in front of a packed Dalymount crowd. My Dad tried to explain that it didn't matter and that I could still win the competition but the damage had been done, I was inconsolable and had lost my focus and concentration, I knew that I had lost the final and went through the motions as best as I could during the rest of the events but deep inside the spark had gone and I failed to recover the necessary points. I stood with my Dad, as the points were all added up still crying my eyes out. All that practice and hard work had been taken away by this cheat of a judge who we later found out was the father of one of the other finalists and was obviously trying to give his boy a better chance, can you believe it! It was his word against this little 12-year-old boy 'me', so we didn't stand a chance of getting it overturned. The announcement was made that a boy from Galway was the winner and he had won a trip to the Bobby Charlton Soccer academy in England. I had finished third and was distraught. Even a dress-up Big Bird couldn't raise a smile from me as I made my way up the steps of the main stand to collect my trophy. It was my first taste of bitterness in relation to football. Maybe looking back it hardened me a little and one thing for sure was that it taught me that I didn't like losing. A well-known future Republic of Ireland International footballer also took part in the competition that day by the name of Steve Staunton. Steve went on to have a terrific professional career and we would cross paths on a couple of occasions some years later.

FOOTBALL BECOMES SERIOUS

The ages between 8 and 12 in Dublin were innocent days when football was played with no pressure and although I was extremely competitive, no thoughts of improving my status in Dublin football had come to mind. This state of mind would change real soon.

My Footballing life was about to turn in a new direction soon after the Coca-Cola final. Myself and my friend Alan Jordan were put forward for under-13 Dublin County soccer trials by our club Tymon Bawn. These trials were a long drawn-out process for selecting the best players in Dublin who would go on to represent the county in the under-14 Kennedy Cup national competition. This group of players would then go on to form the nucleus for the under-15 International team, but that was dreaming for a little kid like me.

We went along for our first trial, which was basically a full-size practice game, where players were sorted into their relevant positions to show what they could do. The selectors watching would then pick out the best players and put them forward to the next trial. The selectors were two men by the name of Joe Nolan and Bob Smith (if my memory serves me right). They would stand beside the pitch writing down the names of those who caught their eye whilst substituting players and giving everybody a good go. The level of football was good, the games being played far more competitively and at a much faster pace than I was used to with Tymon Bawn. The Dublin schoolboy league was the largest in Europe so there was no shortage of keen and eager 12/13 year olds out to impress. For me and Alan, this was a major step up in the standard of football and I no longer found myself the best player on the pitch. Following the first trial, we were advised to look in the Tuesday edition of the Herald newspaper to see whether or not we would be invited to further trials. Come Tuesday we were all nervous to see if we would progress. We scanned the paper and to our delight discovered both mine and Alan's names included for the next trial. The first hurdle had been accomplished. The second trial was to be Alan's last and from there on I was on my own. With every trial completed the standard got better and better. The football was far from fun during these trials as it was all about survival, about striving to be better than the rest. Early lessons in life were being played out. I mean it was pretty basic stuff, if you weren't good enough you were out and your name would no longer appear in the Tuesday Herald, the chance would be gone. I have to say that I really did not enjoy these trials and I would force myself through the whole process. As a boy, I was quite shy around strangers and was very naive in the ways of life, probably like most twelve-year-olds. Sometimes I looked at the Herald on a Tuesday and somewhere inside a voice would say "I hope my name doesn't appear" cause then I wouldn't have to have to suffer that 'fear' feeling that knotted my stomach at the trials. At the same time, I knew I would be very disappointed if I wasn't picked. Strange the way the brain or soul or whatever handles these emotions works. Maybe it was just a nervous thing. The fact was though, I hated the feeling!

What I did do though was give it my best once I was on the football pitch, by competing, battling, and searching out the ball wherever I could. I can honestly say that I never felt I did particularly well at this endless number of trials but for some reason, I kept being picked. After a while I began to get to know some of the lads who were regulars at the trials, people like Curtis Fleming and Eric Carolan from Belvedere Football Club, Alan Birch, and Bobby Hogan from Stella Maris Football Club. I can still recall Eric's fantastic dribbling skills and Bobby's fantastic pace and finishing ability. I remember one day Bobby scoring an identical goal to Marco Van Basten's spectacular effort for Holland in the European Championship finals years later. Maybe Marco was watching the game and learned from Bobby!

The pressure was on to come up to these high standards and it really took every bit of effort from me. I simply had to adjust to the pace of the games. The battle of forcing myself to do something that I wasn't enjoying paid off when finally a squad of players was selected at the end of the season to go away on a weekend coaching course. The venue was Mosman Holiday Camp, which is a coastline holiday resort just north of Dublin. Both the Under 13 and 14 squads were gathered together for the weekend.

The under-14s had already competed in the National Kennedy Cup competition and had easily won the competition in a final at Dalymount Park Dublin. Our squad had been invited to attend the game and I had sat and watched in awe at the way a couple of Dublin players performed. The first was a midfielder by the name of Ricky Mc Evoy. He appeared to have the ball stuck to his feet and would comfortably dribble past defenders like they weren't there. A technique Ricky used that day when confronted by two defenders, was to move the ball from foot to foot quickly as he went through the middle of the defenders. I had never seen this skill and would later practice it and add it to my own repertoire. Ricky and I would later become teammates at Luton Town and he was certainly one of the most talented players I would have the pleasure of playing with. The other guy that day was Ray Kelly. Ray was also from Tallaght and was a 14-year-old legend in Dublin schoolboy football. Although from Tallaght he played for the north of the river side Home Farm, a club considered to be the shop window of Irish football, and had already been for various trials at English league clubs including Arsenal. This was the first time that I saw him play and he was an absolute powerhouse in the middle of the pitch. He was quick, strong, and skillful and had a thunderous shot. I would often see Ray training at our local park in Old Bawn Tallaght. He would seem to do a million laps at pace without getting tired. I learned a lot from watching Ray and was soon working on my own fitness in that park. We were meant to train together one day, a session arranged by a mutual friend, but he didn't show and I was bitterly disappointed and frustrated as trudged off home with my ball under my arm.

I watched in awe as the Dublin team with Kelly and Mc Evoy was awarded the Cup that day by one of my all-time heroes 'sir Bobby Charlton'. For those who don't know, Bobby Charlton was one of the world's greatest-ever footballers. His career spanned the 50s, 60s, and 70s with Manchester United and England and the man was and still is a true legend. I had a video (a new invention at this time) of a documentary featuring Bobby Charlton and I would watch it over and over again, totally enthralled by this man's story. Bobby was famous for his powerful shots, which I would try to emulate through practice, but something else he said in the video really caught my attention at this young age. Whilst being interviewed he was asked to comment on a near-post goal he scored in the 1968 European Cup final. Bobby commented that all he could hear was his coach Jimmy Murph saying, "Near post, get to the near post." Now I was never the tallest kid in the world, so I figured that to score against big defenders I would follow Bobby's advice and get in front of them at the near post, timing my run to meet the ball at pace as it arrived in the box. Boy did it work and through my career many goals were scored on that near post. Bobby Charlton may have been hearing his 'Jimmy Murphy' but I was hearing 'Bobby Charlton'! As I sat right behind Bobby when he awarded the cup to Dublin's captain it was terrific to be on the same ground as the man let alone 5 yards away from him!

The weekend coaching course at Mossman's was my first taste of professional coaching. For the first time, I was faced with grids, bibs, funny rules, and lots of football. We had been through an entire season's worth of trials to get to this stage and here we were the elite of Dublin, being taught how to really play the game. I can't recall being frightened by this weekend in the way I was during the trials. By now I had established myself as a good player within the group and knew everyone's name. John Clarke of Home Farm football club was highly regarded within the squad and I can remember him saying, "The thing about you Aaron is that everyone hates playing against you because you never give up." The words stuck with me and gave me great confidence. For the first time, I realised the main reason I was holding my own amongst Dublin's best, I was a battler.

The weekend was a fantastic success both on the playing field and off. There were two magic moments that occurred which I would like to tell you about. The first happened on the boating lake and involved two of my mates, Paul Mulvaney and Curtis Fleming. Before I tell you the story I should explain that Paul was quite a tall lad, a midfielder with long legs and a good turn of pace. Curtis was the only Black Dubliner I knew and was always a great crack. He would later go on to have a very successful professional career with Middlesborough Football Club in the premiership. Being in a holiday camp, to entertain themselves the lads decided to take a small rowing boat out on the small dirty-looking lake, and for whatever reason I waited for them on the bank. As they meandered their way back to the jetty Paul unexpectedly decided to stand up. On doing so the boat began to gather a rocking motion which is not a good thing if you want it to stay the right way up. "Sit down ya eegit" screamed Curtis as his face began to fill with horror. I'm not sure if Curtis could swim but the expression on his face looked like he didn't want to learn now. By this time

Paul's weight had done too much damage and one side of the boat rose beyond the point of no return bailing out the two lads. Curtis hit the water with a face that could not have looked more terrified if he was falling into the Arctic. 'SPLASH' just as quick as they had gone into the water they jumped back out again. The water unknowingly to all of us was only knee deep!! The lads were drenched and the fearful looks had been for nothing. I fell around the place laughing as Curtis cursed and gave Paul some stick as they dragged the boat towards the shore. It was a priceless moment; I only wish I had a video.

The other magic moment that occurred was when I was voted 'player of the weekend' by the coaches. This was a terrific achievement for me and was totally unexpected. I had missed the last day of coaching through illness, which made it even more amazing that I had won the award. It established me now as one of the leading players in the group. How times were changing. My Tymon Bawn days had to end. I needed to compete at this level week in and week out. A new club had to be sought out.

THE STELLA YEARS

In Ireland club football is the arena where serious football is played. As boys reach the ages of 14 and 15 scouts from top English clubs, based in Ireland, seek out the talented boys and send them over for trials and the like in the UK. The scouts would watch the top clubs in action and in Dublin that meant division A. Somewhere along the line during my trials for Dublin; my Dad was approached by a club called Stella Maris. They were renowned as one of the elite clubs in Ireland and drew players from all over the county to play for them. For me it was like being asked to play for Manchester United such was the step up in standard. We jumped at the opportunity and soon I became a Stella Maris under-14 player. Stella had their own private ground situated in the North side of Dublin in Drumcondra. The pitch was kept in pristine condition by a groundsman by the name of Gerry Lennon. It was surrounded by an iron bar to keep people back from the pitch and was flanked on one side by a high factory wall that ran the length of the pitch. It was an enclosed ground with our own dressing rooms and tarmac training area, which were floodlit during evening training sessions. What's so special about your own dressing rooms I hear you say? Well simply, it was rare that you came across them in Dublin schoolboy football. A big tree or the back of a car was normally the only option for getting changed.

Our manager at Stella was a little stout Dublin guy by the name of John Crilly. John was from Ringsend Dublin, drove an old estate car, and always gave a terrific team talk before we went out to play, with things like "the midfield is the engine room and you lads are like pistons working up and down the pitch". John did a great job and managed to round up a talented bunch of players. Amongst the lads were four of the Dublin squad who all lived in Tallaght, Bobby Hogan Alan Birch later Tommo Price, and myself. He had also pulled in other Dublin players like Paul Mulvaney, the guy who fell in the lake, goalkeeper Andy Farrell, defender Aiden Mooney, and midfielder Justin Devaney.

We trained once a week on a Wednesday night and John in the early days would come across to Tallaght to pick us all up in his estate and then drive us all the way over to Drumconda, which was at least a 45-minute drive. After training he would then drop us home again. I would have hated to see his petrol bill! I'm not sure when but after a while we found ourselves making our own way over to Drumcondra and back. John had obviously thought, "Ah here, I can't keep doing this". If a parent lift wasn't available m e and the lads would meet up at the local bus stop and catch the 77A or the 49 bus into the city, a 40-minute bus ride, and then transfer on to another bus, which would take us out past Drumcondra where we'd walk the last 15 minutes. All in all, it would take us a good hour and a half to two hours to get there for training. Of course, after training the return journey had to be made although sometimes we would be brave and walk into the city on the way home, using a shortcut through back alleys and God knows where else that Bobby Hogan knew. The thing was, none of us cared about traveling, and it was simply what we had to do to play football at the highest level.

My first few games for Stella were tough. Although the trials had prepared me for a step up in pace, when I went into a competitive game it took a little bit of getting used to. My Dad had a chat with John Crilly after the first game and anxiously asked, "Do you think he'll adapt John". "Of course, he will, just needs to adjust to the pace" came back the dismissive reply. John was right, after a few games I was buzzing and Stella was a great success winning many games and challenging for titles and cups. More importantly, I was enjoying my football and had established myself as one of the leading players in Dublin football.

Stella was also the first place I had played where physical training was seen as vital to the success of the team. Harry Volks was the trainer and would happily put us through our paces on a Wednesday night. Harry was a big man with huge biceps and had obviously experienced some good training methods. After a stretch on the half-lit tarmac training area, which was nearly always wet and slippy, Harry would begin the body strengthening with his favourite ritual. He began by swinging his arms in a windmill fashion faster and faster, which of course we had to also do. After a few minutes of this, we would follow his lead, as Simon says, and hold our arms out horizontally at shoulder level. This stance would go on for a few minutes by which time the pain began to creep into the shoulder area and the biceps and triceps in the upper arm. However, this was only the beginning."And small circles" Harry would say as we all moved our aching limbs in slow circling movements trying desperately not to drop our arms below shoulder level "and faster" Harry said as he showed no signs of pain "and the other way" Oh my God the pain was now too much, can't hold on much longer. Lads arms by this stage were dropping in agony but still, Harry was relentless "GET THOSE ARMS BACK UP" He'd shout staring unmercilessly at whoever had failed to keep up. Shrieks and swear words abounded as Harry kept us standing there until finally, he said "and relax".

Aaron Tighe

Shuttle runs would be next. These are short runs that I'm sure everybody who has played football has experienced. We'd sprint to a marker 5 yards away, turn sharply back to where we started, and then sprint to a marker 10 yards away and return, etc etc. This type of running simulates a football field where players will run in short sharp twisting and turning movements This was always exhausting work and made the heart race and lungs suck in the cold night air.

Of course, the football would then come out and we would play 5 a side or some form of training practice. Actual football coaching was limited at the time and that would be carried out more at the Dublin level. Gerry Lennon the groundsman however was very knowledgeable in the game and would sometimes take sessions and coach player's individual techniques and the like. I was like a sponge at the time soaking up every bit of knowledge possible in my quest to be the very best that I could be.

This openness on my part was an innocent characteristic of my teenage years and was something that I really wouldn't lose until my late teens. In fact only in my early twenties would I question rightly or wrongly people who I considered to be in authority, people like managers and coaches. The reason I mention this is that I believe it is important to teach our kids to question things and to speak up if something doesn't feel right. At some stage during the two years I had at Stella Maris, two coaches took me and a couple of boys from Washington DC on a trip up the mountains. The lads were part of an American soccer team who were over in Dublin to play some friendlies whilst taking time out to see the sights. We set off showing the lads the beautiful Wick low Mountains, eventually arriving at a well-known reservoir, where we got out to breathe the air and look at the wonderful scenery. One of the Americans, a blonde guy, was very enthusiastic about everything and was very keen on thinking that he was God's gift to the world. In other words, he was quickly becoming a pain in the arse. "Aaron, race Paul (can't remember the guy's real name) down to the reservoir and back and see who's the fastest" shouted one of the coaches, as we stood at the top of this steep grass incline which stretched about 100 yards down to the water. American Paul of course was up for the challenge and I, being one to go along with what people in authority say, nodded in acceptance. "On your marks, get set, go" the coach shouted and off we sprinted down the steep hill and back with me winning by a whisker. I'd beaten the American but that wasn't to be the end of it. The day being a hot summer day was not the type of day that endears itself to running up and down steep hills, so I was amazed to hear before we had even caught our breath the order "Do it again lads, Do it again" from the coach laughing at the other as if it was a great joke. Now this is where I should have stood up and said "piss off, do it yourself", but being the type that I was I nodded my acceptance and set off down the hill again pumping my legs and arms as fast as I could so as not to lose the race. After that race, the shout was "and again lads, and again". It was at this point that I knew that something wasn't right about the situation and felt like I was being exploited for someone's pleasure. I could see it in their eyes. It had turned from a joke into something else and I didn't like it. I'll let you draw your own conclusions. For me a lesson had been learned, say no if you think it's not right.

LEADERSHIP CHARACTERISTICS

Throughout this time playing for Stella I learned how to become a leader within the team. I was very enthusiastic about the game and was probably the most vocal on the football pitch, encouraging the team and myself to greater efforts and a battling performance. It's amazing really as off the pitch I was pretty shy and quiet but always held the respect of others (at least I think so). I have my family to thank for that characteristic. My brothers Graham and Derek were both individualistic in different ways. Graham was an extrovert and a bright leader and fighter. He always led the charge, in fights or anything that he did. Derek on the other hand was an introvert but behind his shyness lay an intelligent wisdom. My personality has without a doubt developed from both of their characters and lies somewhere in the middle. Obviously, we got that from our upbringing and certain lessons that were taught to us.

An example of this would be when I was around twelve years of age. Ska music was the big thing amongst my friends. For those of you who are wondering what the hell Ska music is, I'll fill you in as best as I can. It was a type of reggae-sounding music that was coming out of England with bands like 'The Specials' and

'Madness'. Of course, like with every craze, kids want to dress like the bands, walk and talk like the bands, and generally look 'cool'. All my friends had gone out and bought the black 'Harrington jacket', which was a must to be in with the crowd. Wanting to be part of the crowd I approached my Dad one day Dad, can I have the money to buy a Harrington jacket?" I asked hopefully. Dad then went into the questioning, "Why do you want one?" "Cause all my friends have them Dad," I said as if it would be the end of the world if the answer was no. "Well son, you are far better off being an individual than just following along with the rest, you'll get far more respect that way," he said wisely, and guess what? He was right! A few months down the road Ska was forgotten about and heavy metal had taken over and let's not go there! Anyway, the point had well and truly sunk in and was a valuable lesson that I have always carried with me. Be yourself and do what you want to do as best as you can. So that is probably part of the reason, leadership skills were gained along the way, and in football that can be useful.

The Stella years were probably the most enjoyable years of my footballing life. I was achieving things at a great rate of knots and it felt good. The nervousness of my early trial days had passed as I established myself as a leading player in Dublin football. My first year at Stella was the year of the Kennedy Cup, the National competition where Dublin took on the rest of the World, well Ireland at least. It was the culmination of all our trials and the reward for our efforts. I took up the centre-midfield position in the team alongside Home Farm's John Clarke and together we murdered the opposition, first County Sligo away and then Limerick in the semifinal at Stella's ground. The final was due to be held at Tolka Park, one of the soccer stadiums in Dublin. However, the pitch, much to our disappointment, was waterlogged and the game was played at Stella's ground. All I can remember was that the rain never stopped during the game but we didn't care, in fact, we loved it. I had my sleeves rolled up and wore blue and white Dublin-coloured sweatbands around my wrists, the in thing at the time. I battled like my life depended on it and in the end, we came away as Champions of Ireland. We had a terrific team spirit in the side and one of my fondest photographs is of me with a couple of teeth missing, looking totally drenched holding the cup aloft in the dressing room after the game. It was a moment of complete satisfaction and pride, a wonderful feeling, and a special time. This group of players had climbed Everest it seemed, by succeeding through all the trials over a two-year period. Together we had formed a solid bond and being from Dublin the Capital of Irish football had dealt with the added pressure of being expected to win. All of these aspects added to the Glory of the result.

DUBLIN, IRELAND & A COUPLE
OF ENGLANDS FINEST

As you can probably tell, football had by this stage, pretty much taken over my life. I still of course went to school and did all the normal things that kids do but my mind was now even more fixed firmly on football. The season 1983/ 1984 was to be the most amazing of my life. Huge achievements were to be made and dreams that I had been having since I was 4 years old were about to come true.

The Dublin training sessions continued this season, only now they had turned into preparations for international matches later in the season. Somewhere along the lines one of Ireland's top coaches Maurice Price became involved in the coaching of the team and Maurice was good. He was the first, what I'd call a professional coach that I had worked with. Maurice enthusiastically explained tactics and positional play as well as prepared us for set pieces etc. For example when our goalkeeper had the ball Maurice coached the full-backs to break wide and deep to receive it whilst encouraging the centre-backs to also play from the back. He also showed the midfield players how to position themselves to receive the ball etc. He coached the team to mark zonally for corners against and attack the space in front of you, all amazingly new concepts to us youngsters. Looking back it amazes me that this was the first real professional coaching that I had received. Certainly, in England, kids receive some excellent coaching from a young age and you don't have to be a potential international to get that coaching. It has been a while since I've been to Ireland, so all I can say is that I hope standards have progressed throughout the game levels. "You are the King of all you survey" Maurice would shout with enthusiasm as he demonstrated creating space and getting your head up to look around the pitch. These were all valuable lessons and I always concentrated on every aspect of his and others' coaching, that way learning not only about my own position but also about everyone else's. Maurice later went on to have a very successful coaching role under Jack Charlton for the full national side during the Republic of Ireland's glory years.

So with Maurice on board and another coach by the name of French also taking up the reigns, standards were improving. Dublin/Ireland training took place on a Monday evening at Stella's ground and then we'd make the trip over for club training on a Wednesday night. The reason I include Dublin and Ireland training as one is down to the fact that virtually all of the Ireland squad were Dublin players, the funny thing is, that some of Ireland's most successful players in recent years have not come from Dublin, people like Manchester Uniteds Roy Keane and Dennis Irwin (both from Cork) and Liverpool's Steven Staunton (Dundalk). Maybe those guys had to work harder to break through and that stood them in good stead going into men's football, just a thought, I could be totally wrong, but it's interesting all the same.

Whilst all this was going on, club football was our bread and butter and at the end of one Stella game, as I emerged from the dressing room, my Dad introduced me to this little Dublin man who was dressed in a smart overcoat and wore a trilby type hat. As we shook hands I thought he was trying to break my hand, such was the tightness of his grip. "Aaron meet Eddie Corcoran, he wants to have a chat with you," said my Dad as he ambled away leaving us alone. A million things were going through my mind like "Who the hell is this guy?" " What does he want?" Why has Dad left us alone?" I was to find out the answers very quickly. "Come on over here," Eddie said as he guided me over to the barrier, which surrounded Stella's pitch. "I've been watching you play for a few games now and I think you've been doing very well I was wondering if you'd like to go over to Luton town and spend a week with them. Now it's not a trial, it's just simply a holiday for you and a chance to spend some time at a first-division football club".

Wow, let's pause it there. I have to explain what those few words spoken by this small, well-dressed Dubliner meant to me. He was asking me to spend a week with an 'English first division football club'. Remember that back in 1983 the first division was the top division in English football and that meant that I would be spending time with people who were on Match of the Day on television, people who appeared in all the football magazines, people who played against Manchester United, people who were professional footballers, people who were living out nearly every schoolboy dream. As he said the words thought of players like Ricky Hill, Paul Walsh, David Moss, and Brian Stein. These were famous footballers that I watched on television. This guy was asking me if I would like to fly to the moon! The emotion of it got to me and I choked, holding back the tears such was the enormity of what he had asked me from somewhere in my throat I managed to produce a sound "I'd love to".

The time was set for a week in November during a mid-term break in school. I packed my bags and excitedly headed off to the airport. I was 14 years old at this stage and met up with a 16-year-old lad by the name of Mark Brearton who was also going over for a ' football holiday'. This certainly was a holiday with a difference. The ones who performed well were asked back and had the opportunity to impress enough to be considered as potential professional footballers. Mark was a nice lad; he had a quietish personality, was fair-haired, and had a strong-looking build. I on the other hand was still a skinny little thing and still very shy. I can't remember too much about getting over to England. I remember flying into Heathrow airport and me and Mark walking out the arrival gate to be met by this guy who gave us a lift to Luton. For me, it was very strange to be back in England. I have lived the last 6 years in Ireland and there is a definite difference in the way the countries look and feel. The first thing you notice is the accent. I had by this stage developed a Dublin accent but it is incredible how much you notice an accent when you arrive in a new country, until of course you get used to it after a couple of days. The other very noticeable difference was the roads. don't ask me why but they just seem different. Maybe it's the colour or the width or the lines, I don't know. The point is I was back in the country I was born in but it felt like a strange place. However, that wasn't a bad feeling. I always loved going back to England, it was where I came from, just as in later years I would love to return to Ireland, as that was also where I came from. I suppose I'm pretty lucky in that respect, I have a number of homes.

On arrival in Luton we were dropped off at our digs, otherwise known as our home for the next week. It was a little terraced house on Poynters Road in the northern suburbs of Luton, where we were looked after by this lovely old lady who showed us to our room, which had only one bed. Ah well, Mark didn't snore! She told us to make ourselves comfortable and then laid out the ground rules, like when dinner and breakfast would be served. We were informed that the following morning we would be picked up to go to training and that was that.

Luton is situated 30 or so miles north of London. It is quite a big town with a cosmopolitan mix of people. It is situated right next to the M1 motorway, which takes you from London to the North of England and is famous for its Airport and probably the fact that the Vauxhall Company has a huge presence with a number of factories and production plants there. It has a large Irish, Italian, and Asian population with the Asian section being made up of

Pakistani, Bangladeshi, and Indian people. Over the last twenty years, the Asian population has settled around the centre of the town virtually making it an Asian country within an English town. In recent years the town has been host to the biggest carnival in Britain, its success deriving itself from the fantastic varying cultures that make up Luton.

The following morning after our arrival about 9.30, there was a knock on the front door, and our lift had arrived. This was it, I was going training with a professional football club and not only that but one of the leading teams in the country, even if they had just been thrashed by the Champions Liverpool 6 -0 at Anfield. Luton Town football club had up until this stage been one of those clubs that were on the periphery of my football knowledge. They would be like Bolton or Fulham in today's premier League. I knew some of their players and knew of their manager David Pleat, mainly because he did a famous run and dance the season before when the club managed to stay up on the last day of the season but apart from that very little. I also knew that they played an attractive passing style of game because I had watched them on TV and it was always good to watch. They had in fact been promoted as Champions to Division One in 1982 and were now playing only their second consecutive season in the top flight. However, the club had previously had various spells in the top division with the club's best success arriving in 1958 when they reached the FA Cup final, narrowly losing to Nottingham Forest.

The guy picking us up that morning was a young professional at the club by the name of Gary Parker. All I can recall about his car was that it was white and it was sporty. Gary drove us up and down the narrow Luton roads winding his way in and out of parked cars that allow room for only one car to get through, until about twenty minutes later we arrived at the football ground. He showed us into the building, guiding us down various corridors, and eventually showing us the away team dressing room. Just before we entered the dressing room we were greeted by this loud brash Scottish voice "Hey lads, how ya doing" Coming towards us was this tall, slim, sharp-featured guy who looked about 40 odd and as tough as nails. "Hi, I'm John Moore the youth team coach. Stick your bags in there and go and have a look at the pitch until we go training" he said in a friendly but efficient manner. We did as he said, throwing our bags in the changing room and then making our way down the player's tunnel and out onto the pitch. I must tell you, there is something very special about walking down the tunnel towards a football pitch. Even when there is no game and nobody around, you still get a tinge of expectancy and excitement as you begin to see the grass from underneath the roof of the tunnel, gradually filling your vision as you reach the exit and walk out into the day with the terraces and stands around you. On this day it was more special as it was my first time. Luton's ground certainly isn't huge and was built many moons ago but still had that air of history and passion that football grounds echo when they are empty. Me and Mark hung around for a while down by the pitch side heeding the warning signs, which read 'Keep off the grass'. As no one had come to get us for training we took a walk up the main stand to get a better view of the surroundings. About half an hour later we decided we had better go back inside and find out what was going on. So we walked back up the tunnel and back into the dressing room where we sat around waiting once more for someone to come and tell us what was happening. After about ten minutes the door bashed open. "There you are, you'd better get your arses moving or you'll be straight back on the next plane to Dublin" bawled this little fiery fortyish-year-old man. "I've just taken all the lads training and have had to come back for you two. Where were you?" he barked obviously angry at the fact He'd forgotten us. "We were out looking at the pitch" we replied, but he wasn't listening as he said, "come on then get a move on". Jim McCabe the bus driver huffed and puffed all the way to the training ground as me and Mark anxiously sat on the team coach, wondering what we'd be doing at training and whether or not we really were going to be put on the first plane back to Dublin, I mean how embarrassing would that be, we'd only just arrived.

As we entered the training ground, we could see the players already playing on one of the many pitches. We got down off the bus and ran the 100 yards or so to where the coaches stood, watching the game in progress. "Ah there you are, what happened to you?" asked John Moore in his strong Scottish accent. "We were waiting down by the pitch" we replied, repeating what we had told Jim the bus driver. "Ah never mind hang on a minute and we'll get you involved," said John. As I stood and watched the players in there five side game, I began to recognise some of the faces and in particular David Pleat the manager who was shouting instructions at the side of the pitch.

David Pleat for those of you unfamiliar with the name had brought Luton Town into the top division in England and was highly respected in the game for his knowledge and ability to get his teams to play attacking one and two-touch football. At this period and for a number of seasons he would be tipped as a future England manager. During a very successful period as manager at Luton he made his name and then continued that success with Tottenham Hotspur, where he molded a team filled with stars like Glen Hoddle, Ossie Ardiles, and Chris Waddle into a 4,5,1 formation. That team's success largely derived from the goalscoring feats of the solitary forward Clive Allen, who scored 50-odd goals in one season. However personal affairs appeared in newspapers which led to his departure despite his success Mr. Pleat then went on to have spells at Leicester City, Luton again, Sheffield Wednesday, and finally with the twists of time back to Tottenham as director of football. The England position had eluded him and at a time when he would have been a prime candidate, the position instead went to his rival Graham Taylor, an introducer and advocate of the long ball game in England. Mr. Pleat had major effects on my life as his decisions changed the direction and path of my career on 3 significant occasions, which I will explain as we move through my story.

Some of the skills on view as I watched the game amazed me, particularly one of the most well-known Luton players Paul Walsh. Paul was a centre-forward with incredible close ball control and tricks to beat opponents. I watched in awe as He'd nutmeg Brian Horton the Luton Captain and tease big defenders like Paul Elliot before flicking the ball with the outside of his foot to a teammate. This was truly incredible stuff. Paul would later go on to play for the great Liverpool team of the eighties and England amongst others. After a while our chance had come. David Coates, the first team coach set up a small 20-yard by 20-yard pitch and asked me and Mark to pair up and play against two Luton players. As we prepared ourselves to attack, our opponents were introduced, Ricky Hill and one other who I can't recall. Please bear in mind here that I was 14 years old and as excited as someone who had just won the lottery, so my memory is doing quite well. Ricky Hill I must tell you was a player that I knew from Match of the Day on television. He was what I would call a football star and here I was being thrown a ball so that I could take him on and try and get past him, Wow, it doesn't get much better than this. I mean this was like David and Goliath with me playing the role of David for real. Well, I'm pleased to tell you that I gave it a good go, but I don't think I got past Ricky, but what do you expect, the man was an England international!

The week spent at Luton Town was a schoolboy's dream and maybe even some adult's dream come true. At no stage did I consider it to be a trial and arrived with the mindset of ' I'm going to enjoy myself and lap up every minute'. The week's enjoyment went from strength to strength with the highlight arriving on Thursday. Luton was due to play fellow first division rivals QPR away at Loftus Road, a ground which had recently become home to England's first artificial playing surface, otherwise known as the 'plastic pitch'. Mark and I were both invited to travel down with the players and staff on the first team coach for a training session on the pitch. This was the usual thing to do for away teams so that they could get a feel for the surface before the game on a Saturday.

When we arrived at the ground we were escorted into the dressing rooms where two teams were picked to play a full-scale practice match. The teams were basically the first team, who were going to play on Saturday versus the reserve team, but the game was taken seriously and both teams were fully kitted out in the white home strip and the orange away strip. As I expected, I wasn't included in the teams and was happy just to be a spectator of the day's events. However, I got changed and joined in the warm-up on the plastic pitch. The game got underway with Mark included in the reserve team and I happily sat on one of the benches in awe at the fact I had just been kicking a ball around on QPR's pitch. One player who scored a fantastic chipped goal that day was a Luton youngster by the name of Mark Stein who later went on to have a very successful career at Luton, Stoke, and Chelsea amongst others.

With 15 minutes to go, I heard David Pleat shout out "Aaron on you go, play left-side midfield". Was I hearing correctly? I was only 14, surely he doesn't want me to play. As my thoughts were racing I heard "Go on son, on you go" My heart skipped a beat as I ran onto the pitch joining the reserve team and playing my first ever football at a first-division football ground. I felt like producing a smile from ear to ear but remained focused on doing the best that I could do. After a few minutes, I received my first touch of the ball receiving a pass from one of the midfielders. I immediately turned on the ball and began to dribble the ball towards the Luton defender Kirk Stevens, alias 'Basher', trying to drop my shoulder and go past him with the ball before being forced back to pass. Wow what a feeling, this was the best holiday, I wouldn't mind having some more of this!

Aaron Tighe

On the bus back to Luton, David Coates the first team coach idled up the aisle and in his amusing enthusiastic manner roared out "Son, what did you think you were doing when you dribbled the ball at Kirk Stevens, don't you know who he his? He' s not called Basher for nothing you know, nobody tries to dribble past Basher". The players laughed at the comment, as David winked at me and patted me on the head in an acknowledgment of well-done son. My fifteen minutes had made an impression and it felt good.

The week came to an end and before we knew it we were back on the plane to Dublin. To cut a long story short, I had made a terrific impression and Luton wanted me to return at the earliest opportunity for further training. The seed had been sewn. Unfortunately, Mark never made it back and I never managed to see him again. Friendships are made quickly in football and then you move on to other teams and ventures losing touch as quickly as you made friends. One of the things that always intrigues me is looking at a team photo a few years old and comparing it to a current one. You very quickly notice how much it has changed, life hey! The week in Luton was an awesome experience for me. I kept a diary of the five days noting the details of the training sessions we took part in and the famous players that I had rubbed shy but proud shoulders with. Unfortunately, I have since misplaced that diary, a shame but in any case, the memory is enough.

When I returned to Dublin, I was a changed person. It is truly wonderful how much your state of mind can change through confidence. At both school and at football, I now had this knowledge that I had impressed at an English top-division football club, which meant I could hold my own with anyone. All of a sudden in matches with both Stella and Dublin I could run that little bit faster, go past players with the ball a little bit easier, and tackle that little bit stronger. Nothing seemed impossible and all down to that word ' confidence'. If only we could bottle the stuff. I have in adult life read numerous books that preach the gospel of positive thinking and having confidence in yourself, but in my experience, I have never been able to generate true confidence myself, it has always come from a manager praising me, or a goal being scored or an action that I have done being recognised by others. True confidence is like a rush of adrenalin, everything is that bit sharper and focused. A good manager learns how to balance between raising players' confidence whilst not encouraging overconfidence or laziness.

The months from January 1984 to July 1984 saw me change from a boy to a young man. Firstly the Dublin/Ireland squad was now in full training and matches were arranged for us to play against North Wales and Belfast. These were considered warm-up matches for the full internationals, which were the real carrots at the end of the stick. I proudly captained the team in both of the games and found them to be a real challenge, particularly against the Welsh lads who were very strong physically. After the game against North Wales, both teams were invited to a Dublin Hotel for a post-match dinner with the various dignitaries of both the Irish and Welsh associations. Towards the end of dinner, speeches were in full swing as senior committee members spoke about the wonderful standard of players on display and how great the future of football looked for both Dublin and North Wales etc. Of course with young 14 and 15-year-olds, the information goes in one ear and out of the other and this was certainly the case with me until the unthinkable happened. "Can I ask the captain of Dublin Aaron Tighe to come up and present this pennant to north Wales" said the guy on the mic who stood at the head table gazing out into the sea of faces. A big cheer went up from my teammates as I nervously made my way up to the top table. Embarrassed to be standing up there in front of everyone, I coped by remembering that all I had to do was hand over a pennant. The problem arose as the Dublin lads started chanting "speech, speech". As I mentioned before, I was very shy as a kid, and getting me to say boo off the football field was hard enough, let alone make a speech. "Good idea," said the man holding the mic as he reached it out towards me forcing me to take hold of it. "Well, I errrrrr" All of a sudden my brain wasn't capable of forming words. I had forgotten how to talk. Eventually, after a few stammers, my brain reverted to the vocabulary of a four-year-old and I managed to thank North Wales for playing us. It was an embarrassing end to a great day but all in good fun.

The friendlies and training sessions were coming to an end as our first full under-15 international approached. I can remember in the years leading up to this, watching England's schoolboy team play live matches on television at Wembley Stadium against Scotland and West Germany. I remember thinking how amazing it would be to be playing at that level. The boys looked so strong and fit and would score some cracking goals. A goal by a young Mark Falco always stuck in my mind. Mark Falco later went on to have a fantastic career with Tottenham. The thing is, here I was preparing to captain my country the Republic of Ireland in the same level of game 'an international', how far I'd come from the 'green' of Banbury to the green of Ireland.

On the Friday before the match against Wales took place, it was school as normal for me. I had some great friends in Old Bawn Community School such as Ivan, Skiv "Goldsberry, Eoin, Porky" Power, and Tony "Noctor" Noctor, who although not serious football players would still join me out on the outdoor basketball court come wind rain or shine at break time for a football match, typically using just a tennis ball with our steel capped shoes scraping across the tarmac court as we slipped and slid to control the ball.

On this day just before the bell went for going home, a crackling sound came from the tannoy speaker system in the corner of the classroom. The headmaster's voice bellowed "It's a special day tomorrow for one of our pupils Aaron Tighe, who will be representing Ireland at football. We would like to all wish him well, good luck Aaron". The crackle then signifies that the tannoy was off. A round of applause then followed in my class with lots of wishes of good luck. This was really happening. It was funny cause I really didn't think that anyone in my school even knew about my football career. Football wasn't considered to be a major sport in the school. It ranked way down the list behind athletics, Gaelic football, and table tennis, all three of which I was involved in school teams at some stage. So this was a nice surprise.

Preparations for the international were very professional with Maurice Price and Manager Brian Kerr getting us ready for action with tactics all worked out and the team selected. The team was basically the Dublin side with two/three additions from Cork and Limerick, such was the strength of the Dublin side. We knew that we were up against a very strong Welsh team, which had 6 players who had played Internationals the year before and therefore had plenty of experience and strength. In the Ireland newspapers, we were seen as the underdogs, which added to the tension of the team, as none of us had played at this level. Although we had trained together for two years through the Dublin trials, Kennedy Cup successes, friendlies against North Wales, Belfast, and Dublin's finest senior teams, nothing compared to an international. This thought was very much in our minds as we prepared for the big day.

On the morning of the game, the squad gathered at the venue 'Whitehall', an amateur venue that only had one area of terracing on one side of the pitch. Once again we had been disappointed by the venue. The game was supposed to take place at Dublin's premier soccer ground Dalymount Park but a waterlogged pitch put an end to that. Instead this International event, the biggest game of our careers took place in a very poor venue. don't get me wrong, at the time we didn't care. The fact that we were playing at all was a fantastic feeling, but looking back now as an adult and as a coach, this game should have taken place at a special venue to promote the importance of the game. A professional atmosphere around football breeds a professional attitude and a desire for people to play the game. The thousands of cheering kids who came to watch the game wouldn't have been impressed with the surroundings. Who knows maybe we lost some kids of the future on that day?

We gathered to have a look at the pitch and get a feel for this strange place. Although we were playing at home, we may as well have been playing in Wales, as we never got to train on the pitch or get used to the surroundings. However, we all looked good, dressed in Green v-neck jumpers with the Irish emblem over the breast and identical dark green ties and trousers. Maybe the ground we were playing in was crap but we still felt like a team and we were still very much buzzed up to represent our country.

After some photos were taken, one of the coaching staff pulled me to one side. "Aaron we've been thinking of giving the captaincy to John Clarke, we want to allow you to concentrate on your game as we think that we'll get the best out of you that way, is that okay?" "Yes no problem," I said quickly even before what he had said had actually sunk in. Now let's hold it there and think about those words that were said. At the time as I have mentioned before, I was a pretty shy kid off the pitch and wouldn't say boo to a goose. I was also a kid who would go along with anything someone in authority would say and therefore naturally the only answer I would give to the question was yes. Also, bear in mind that I had been Captain of the team for the whole season which culminated in these internationals and I was the most vocal and natural leader of the team. That was the reason I had been captain for the entire season. I hope you're following me here. Now suddenly, a couple of hours before the kick-off of the biggest game in my career, I was relieved of the captain's armband, why? To this day I will never know. I have my theory but it is only a theory. International matches draw scouts from all the top clubs in England. In football there are lots of political circles, Captains are Captains because they are considered the most important player on the pitch, the leader! Do I need to say more? I may be completely off the track here and perhaps the decision was made honestly and no disrespect to John Clarke who was a fine player and friend but I was the Captain of that team. During the aftermatch dinner at a Dublin Hotel, Joe Nolan, who was a Dublin official, approached me. Joe had put the initial squad together. "Meet Aaron Tighe the Irish Captain," he said to the man he was introducing to me. As I shook hands I replied, "Sorry Joe I wasn't captain today". "What do you mean you weren't Captain, course you were Captain, I watched the game, don't let anybody tell you different". Joe's words have always stayed with me and got me thinking that maybe there was something a little bit strange about the whole affair. I can honestly say it was only after the game that I thought about it. Prior to the game I was totally focused.

The small Whitehall ground was packed with people as we lined up and proudly stood with chests stuck out listening and singing along to the Irish national anthem. It was a packed crowd that was spilling onto the pitch in the cramped environment and was the most people I had ever played a football match in front of. This all added to the excitement and motivated me to do my very best. The game kicked off and from the very start, we knew we were in for a tough ride. The Welsh lads were a big powerful team and very physical. I loved the battle and straight away got stuck in as best as I could.

The Welsh had a lad playing that day up front who caused us almighty problems by the name of Paul Lewis. Paul and I would unknowingly become teammates within a few months at Luton and he had the most deceiving body swerve that I had ever seen. I can recall one of my first training sessions with Paul where we were pitted one against one outside the box, with the attacking player trying to score. Paul attacked me first and as he approached I assumed my low downside on a defensive posture, Paul, in an instant rolled one leg up and over the ball, shape to go to my right but instead switched his balance going to my left, leaving me standing like an idiot as he scored the goal. The coach David

Aaron Tighe

Coates congratulated Paul on his skill and success, and I being the competitor that I was, was determined to get him the next time. This time Paul approached me doing the same leg-over trick but instead to the opposite side which I read, my mind saying "Got ya" but just as I went for the ball he switched weight and footing and breezed around me on the other side. "Aaron watch the ball" came the shout from David Coates the coach. The problem was, I was watching the ball but still couldn't stop him. Paul was a great centre-forward and a good guy. At the end of his 2 - year apprenticeship at Luton, he went to see the manager at the time John Moore. John offered him a wage that was calculated around the same as he was earning as an apprentice because as a pro you had to pay for your own digs and expenses etc. Paul said that he needed more and John told him he could take it or leave it, so Paul stuck to his guns and left it. It was a very disappointing outcome and I recall that after having a few trials elsewhere Paul left the professional game, a real shame, as he was a gifted player.

Despite our battling efforts and the screams of our supporters the Welsh and Paul Lewis in particular beat us on the day 2 - o. However, despite the defeat we all thoroughly enjoyed the whole occasion. We were now international footballers albeit under 15 internationals and it felt really good. Bring on the next game was the shout. Before we knew it, we were playing our second international against Northern Ireland in Belfast. It was my first visit to the North and we traveled up as a team on the train. Having lived in Ireland for the past 6 years or so, it was strange to see Union Jack flags flying high over the towns as we passed through, I mean we were still in Ireland? The other thing, that told me, this place was a bit different was when RUC (Northern Irish police) walked down the train holding machine guns. I think it was the first time I had ever seen a real gun and it certainly created an atmosphere of fear. I remember thinking how lucky we were to live in the South! I don't mean to be rude but that was my feeling at the time. I had only traveled for a couple of hours and all of a sudden people were carrying guns, scary stuff. The game was an eventful one, with Northern Ireland supporters throwing bottles and things toward our goalkeeper Andy Farrell, can you believe it in an Under 15 game! The North led 2 - 0 at one stage only to see us claw our way back to draw 2 - 2. It was a battling performance and when the final whistle went I had to hold back the tears as my proud emotions came to the surface. There is something about representing your country that is very powerful and emotive. It comes from deep in your heart and when you succeed and do a good job, there is an enormous amount of pride that can be felt. Even when I watch the television and see someone succeeding in a sporting event for their country, I feel emotional, maybe because I've felt it to a smaller extent in my career and can relate to these people. The result against Northern Ireland on this occasion was a comeback against the odds at the time and therefore was a great achievement for us. The other thing was we had come together and produced a good result after the disappointment of losing to Wales. The trip back home was a good one.

Not only had the internationals been a terrific experience but once again they had put it in the shop window for the scouts of England. After the game against Wales, a scout representing the great Chelsea football club approached my Dad. He claimed that I had been the man of the match and offered me a one-week trial at Chelsea FC. Chelsea a big London club, at the time was flying high in the English second division and was regular on TV's Match of the Day or The Big Match with stars like centre-forwards Kerry Dixon and David Speedie, the only players that I could recall at the time. I understood that Chelsea was a pretty big London club but didn't know too much about them. That was soon to change.

CHELSEA BOUND

Once again I excitedly found myself on a plane heading for Heathrow London. This time I was on my own albeit with a little bit of experience under my belt. The Chelsea trip was exciting but didn't have the same innocence about it that I felt when I first went across to Luton. This time round I had a better understanding of what I was going for. On arrival in London, I was met at the airport by a young-looking professional guy by the name of Gwyn Williams, who introduced himself as Chelsea's youth development officer. When we got to Gwyn's car I was introduced to some lads whom Gwyn had already picked up and was happily told that we were heading directly to the training ground, no hanging around this time. On the way, he made a diversion and picked up another player who squeezed into the front seat with me. Squashed in, we headed for Chelsea's training ground, which is situated right next to Heathrow airport, so close in fact that you feel you could reach up and touch the low-flying aircraft. As we arrived and walked towards the storied long bricked clubhouse, Gwyn asked "Aaron do you know Pat who was sitting with you in the front seat?" "No" I replied. I later found out that Pat was in fact Pat Nevin, one of Chelsea's star players and a Scottish international at that! I carried my gear inside the dressing rooms, got changed, and nervously raced out towards a bunch of footballers that were getting warmed up at the far side of the ground. As I approached the group I realised that there were no other kids there, just senior players. Instantly in the group, I recognised Kerry Dixon and David Speedie along with the coach John Hollins, who had been a valuable member of my playing card collection. John had been a famous Chelsea player in their glory days and was now first-team coach. Without any introductions, I joined in the training session. The Chelsea players must have been thinking "what's this kid doing training with us?" and I was wondering the same thing! Fortunately for me, Ireland's school holidays happened to fall at different times to England's hence the reason why I was the only kid on trial at the time.

After a quick warm up John Hollins asked 2 of the players to pick teams for a game. This method of picking teams for anything can be a daunting task if you are not that great at whatever game you are about to play. Even when you are great, there is still that feeling of 'God don't leave me till the last, please' it's particularly worse when you are amongst your peers or mates. Whoever gets picked first is considered the best, the rest of you, well your just not that important! On this occasion as the teams were being picked, expectedly, the kid was left to last, that was me of course. As the picker turned away he got an earful from one of the lads who said, "You shouldn't have left the kid till last". The truth was though that I didn't care, it was just great to be there and anyhow, how could they pick me, they hadn't even seen me play! from the word go in the small-sided game, I got stuck in and passed well whenever I got the ball. I was holding my own with the big boys and it felt good. Pat Nevin who I had been sitting within the front seat of the car was sensational in the training session, with the ball sticking to his feet like glue as he danced and weaved his way around players, from that moment on I was a Pat Nevin fan.

After training, I was taken with a few Scottish lads to a hotel nearby in a fashionable part of London. It was one of those

Chelsea-style white buildings, a hotel owned by Ray W i lk ins parents apparently and I was a huge Ray W i lk ins fan. Ray Wilkins was a Manchester United footballer at the time, which gained him hero status in my eyes. Ray had come through the ranks at Chelsea and was a terrific England international, so to stay at his parent's hotel was a bonus. I shared a single room with the three other lads and God knows how we all squeezed in but we did. Being older they were asked to look after me and the lads were great.

In the mornings we'd catch the bus to Chelsea's home Stamford Bridge and either train there on the main pitch or at the Heathrow training ground. Stamford Bridge was huge compared to Luton Town's ground and was a real thrill to train at, the towering main stand rising high above you in an intimidating but thrilling sight. After a few training sessions, Gwyn Williams had found me a nickname and was constantly calling me 'Liam' after the great Irish International Liam Brady. Liam Brady had been one of my favourite players as a kid. He was a left-footed player who had reached world-class levels with performances for Arsenal and Juventus in particular. In fact Brady had helped Juventus win the Italian title only to be sold to make way for Michelle Platinithe French maestro. In my eyes, there was little to choose between the two of them, but there you go! Anyway as I was saying I had this new nickname and if Chelsea football club were comparing me to the great Liam Brady, well that was good enough for me.

The rest of the week at Chelsea was great fun. Apart from training with the first team squad I also got to hang around the ground and really get to know how the players act and see the kind of lifestyle that they had. I also got an insight into the role of the apprentice and the jobs that they had to undertake, which I'll talk about in more glorious detail a bit later! Gwyn Williams was great at Chelsea and although he hadn't even seen me play a match, could see the potential that I had via the training sessions. One day he took me and a few apprentices into an indoor gymnasium-type place called the 'shed', at least I think that's what it was called. It was situated near the entrance to Stamford Bridge behind the main stand. Gwyn set up a few training sessions which involved passing the ball against the wall using the instep and outside of the foot, along with heading against the wall and just general ball control tasks. These were all second-nature techniques for me, which was a real bonus and impressed Gwyn. Here was this 14-year-old performing a lot better than the apprentices, showing close ball control and an ease with the ball. Of course, the reason for this came from the fact that virtually my entire childhood had been spent kicking a ball against a wall. There is no better way to feel the ball, and gain close control and passing skills. I would recommend it to every kid who has an interest in football. Apart from practice, it simply feels good to do it and to this day I would be quite content spending hours just tapping a ball against a wall using different spins and techniques on the ball.

A treat was in store for me on the Friday evening of my visit, similar to the one I had experienced with Luton at QPR. Chelsea had a top-of-the-table clash away at Manchester City. The game was a big one as the season was drawing to a close and the winners were likely to go on and gain promotion to the top division in England. The game was being shown live on television, which added a certain edge to the atmosphere. The beauty of all this was that I was invited to travel up to Manchester on the director's coach and watch the game. The luxurious coach with televisions and the like seemed a long way from the days my Dad would take me on the back of his Honda 50 to Stella Maris matches and Dublin trials.

We arrived at the ground and I found my way to my seat, excited by the fact that I was back at Manchester City's ground. The last time I had been there was as an adoring football fan who took blades of grass as a memento. Today I was a guest of the club who I had been training all week with, the players that I had trained with were out on the pitch, this was fantastic stuff! I can recall the atmosphere at the game is terrific and I thoroughly enjoyed the game, particularly when Chelsea's Paul Canonville scored two goals (I think it was two) to win the game 2 - 0.

After the game, Gwyn told me that I would be traveling back with the team rather than the directors and gave me directions for the team bus. Excitedly I clambered my way up the steps of the bus and sat down near the front watching the highlights of the game, which were showing on the television situated high in the centre-front of the aisle. The first player to get on the bus was Chelsea defender Colin Lee but after such a great win I was surprised to see that he looked a bit peeved off. As he sat down I said, "Great win, well done" to which he replied, "Yeah thanks but I've just called the wife, and apparently the commentators were giving me some stick". Unhappily he sat down and not much more was said.

The fact that I was sitting having a conversation albeit a short one with Colin Lee may not appear all that special a moment, unless you were of the knowledge that as a 6/7 year old, me and my pal David Primrose were walking back from a Banbury United game when we were brought to a halt outside an electrical stores shop window. The reason being that the results of the day's fixtures were being shown by BBC on one of the televisions displayed in the window. David was as I mentioned earlier a fanatical Tottenham supporter and so we waited for their result to show on TV. After a while, a picture of their centre-forward 'Colin Lee' was shown and the result 9 - 0 appeared. David jumped up and down with the good news and happily, we made our way home. Later we found out that Colin Lee had scored 4 of the goals on his debut and was a real hero. Now you may understand why having that short conversation with the very same Colin Lee on the Chelsea team bus was a special moment for me!

The players rolled onto the bus and in a jubilant atmosphere, we headed south. John Hollins the Chelsea coach made sure I was well watered passing on the lemonade bottle after he and a few others had had a slurp. This was great stuff, I mean John Hollins used to be on my picture cards! Now we were sharing a lemonade bottle!

More traveling occurred the following morning when I was asked to attend the Chels ea reserves match played at Southampton's ground "The Dell". A special moment occurred as I helped the apprentices unload the kit off the bus, a few kids hurried over with autograph books in hand "Can I have your autograph please" asked one "Oh I'm only on trial" I said, a little bit embarrassed, "that's alright, you may be famous one day" the kid said. With that, I wrote my first autograph.

Before I left Chelsea and headed for home, Gwyn introduced me to the manager at the time, a guy by the name of John Neal. It was a brief hello as he was obviously a busy man, but I thought it was a nice touch. Gwyn did a terrific job and I was really comfortable at the club. Afterward, Gwyn asked me what I thought of the club and how it compared to Luton Town "It's much bigger" I replied. "No it's not Liam, it's got a similar size squad and the same level of opportunity," he said positioning the club as the place to choose. Gwyn was right in trying to sell the club to me. Although I had a terrific week there, I didn't feel comfortable with the thought of leaving home to come to the big city of London and be part of what appeared to be a big club. I mean Chelsea at the time had not had any success in years and had a lesser team in ability than Luton, so opportunities would probably come sooner at Chelsea, but something inside was making me feel more comfortable with Luton Town. The thing was, nobody had even asked me to play for them yet but the signs were certainly there that this would be the next step.

STILL A MAN UTD FAN

A little bit earlier in this season, Manchester United had qualified for the Quarterfinals of the Cup Winner's Cup and were set to play the mighty Barcelona of Spain. They had qualified the season before by beating Brighton after a replay in the FA Cup final. My Dad had taken me over to Wembley for the game, a magical experience, as it had been my first visit to Wembley Stadium London. My Uncle Terry from St Albans, a town just outside London had got us tickets through his job with the Daily Mirror newspaper. Dad along with my cousin John and me set off for Wembley and was excited at the prospect of the occasion. The seats we had were excellent as we sat in the same section as players' relatives like Bryan Robson's Mum and Dad and one of my Man Utd heroes Martin Buchan. The match that day took an unexpected twist with the underdog Brighton taking the lead. Utd soon drew level with a fantastic long-distance shot by midfielder Ray Wilkins and the game eventually finished in a disappointing 1 - 1 draw.

The funny part of the story is that the following afternoon my team Stella Maris had an important match against St Kevins, a local rival situated on the north side of Dublin. Knowing the importance of the game, we forfeited the opportunity to go and watch the FA Cup final replay and caught an early morning train from St Albans to Hollyhead where we boarded the ferry to Dublin. We had measured that we would have a couple of hours to spare in Dublin before the match kicked off and that we should make it in time quite comfortably. However, of course, when you need everything to go smoothly, life's little challenges arrive to test us. The boat was delayed by two hours, which left us with no time to spare to get to the football match. On arrival in Dun Laoghaire harbour Ireland, we raced down the gangway, bags in hand desperate to get to the game on time. As we passed the customs desk the uniformed man's hand behind the desk rose up, signaling us like sheep to stop at his command, so that he could go through our personal belongings. Well, you can imagine our faces and thoughts as he took his time to finish his search. Once finished a quick sarcastic thank you from my Dad and we were running again, this time through the exit towards my brother Derek who was waiting outside with Dad's car. Once in the car, the dash was on. We had about twenty minutes to get from the south of Dublin to the North of Dublin, which was a near impossibility. While the car screeched left to right and swung around bends on two wheels, I somehow managed to put on my football kit, which Derek had brought with him. With minutes to spare, we pulled up at the St Kevin's football pitch, opened the doors, and dashed across the park to where I could see the team gathered. At this stage, we had been traveling for something like 8 hours but I was still ready to play and geared up for the game. As we approached the pitch, our manager John Crilly was walking towards us with his arms crossing over each other in front of him, like a boxing referee signaling the end of about as a boxer lies flat out on the canvas. "It's off" John shouted "You what?" shouted my Dad. "It's off, they've called it off". Well, my Dads face was a picture and so was mine.

Man Utd went on without us to win the replay 4 - 1 on the Tuesday following, despite Brighton's heroic captain and England international Steve Foster returning to the team after injury.

Anyway, as I was saying, that win had put Man U into Europe and the team successfully worked its way to a quarterfinal appearance against the mighty Barcelona of Spain. Utd lost the first leg in Spain 2 - 0, a bad result but not impossible to recover from. However, Barcelona did have two of the world's greatest footballers playing for them at the time. First was a German midfielder called Bernd Schuster, who was inspirational to watch, and secondly was the maestro himself Argentina's Diego Maradona. Diego in my opinion was and still is the greatest-ever footballer. If you leave out his off-the-field antics and just look at his performances over the years at the very highest level, he was truly a football genius. Now I know that Pele, Cruyff, Best, and a few more are up there as well, but Maradonna achieved his greatness in an era of man-for-man marking and tight defenses tactically equipped with the knowledge of how to shut an individual player out of a game. Despite this Maradonna still scored amazing individual goals and won titles for his clubs, and the World Cup for his country. The individual goal he scored against England in the 86 - world cup has got to be the greatest goal ever scored and it was scored at the very highest level. This occasion wasn't the first time that I had seen Maradonna in action. A few years earlier my mate Alan Jordan and I went along with his Dad to a friendly international between Ireland and Argentina at Lansdowne Road in Dublin. I was so small I could only see a quarter of the pitch where one of the goals stood. I caught glimpses of the young Maradonna but my best memory of that game was of Ireland's Manchester Utd player Ashley Grimes cracking home a long-distance drive.

For the Barcelona game, my Dad secretly organised two tickets for us and I would have been totally in the dark if it weren't for my 'impossible to keep a secret' bless her Mum. Mum blurted out the secret a day or so before we were due to depart for Manchester.

The difficult thing was that I had to still pretend that it was a glorious surprise. My acting skills were going to be brought to the fore. On the evening before the game, My Dad explained to me that he had received a phone call saying that there was an Ireland training session and we had to leave straight away. Of course, instead of arriving at the diversionary training venue, we arrived at Dun Laoghaire harbour. "What are we doing here?" I asked Dad in a very believable manner. Excitedly Dad replied, we're not going training, we're going to see Man U play!" After the look of surprise on my face and hugs of thanks, we set off on the ferry bound for Old Trafford Manchester. By the way, to this day my Dad still thinks that he truly surprised me, but he should have known better with Mum around.

The atmosphere inside Old Trafford was electric. When the game got underway, the tension and apprehension around the ground smothered you, as if you were about to set off on a brand new roller coaster ride, where you just didn't know what was going to happen. United couldn't afford to concede an away goal. If they did they would have to score 4 goals and that was unlikely against Barcelona. Whenever Barcelona got the ball, all attention turned to Maradonna and thankfully United swarmed him giving him little time and space. Schuster on the other hand had a great game and was fantastic to watch in the midfield. United gradually took a stranglehold on the game and when they scored their first goal, I swear the roof of the stadium lifted off its hinges with the roar of the crowd. I could see the team physically grow in confidence after that and United went on to grab two more, the scorers Captain extraordinaire Bryan Robson and Irish international Frank Stapleton. Despite some anxious moments with Maradonna and friends, United held on to win 3 - 0 and hence go through to the semifinals of the tournament. It was to be my last visit to Old Trafford and the end of my childhood love affair with Manchester United. Attention was now turning to the professional club that I would represent, Luton Town.

DECISIONS, DECISIONS

" Like a river flowing we don't quite know where we're going to, just stay in l ine keep in with the rest. Dream your dreams yeah stay in that scene and hope for the best, things will work out in the end"

— Aaron Tighe "Still not Satisfied" Copyright © 1990

"**A**re you going to sign for us Aaron, because we need to know quickly?" asked David Coates in a no-messing manner. The phone had rung in my Mum and Dad's upstairs bedroom a few minutes earlier and I was on my own in the house at the time. On picking up the receiver I heard the Luton First team coach at the other end. Nervous and a little bit scared I replied "Mmmm I don't know Mr Coates".

The time for a decision was drawing near and Mum and Dad had been talking to both Luton and Chelsea about my future. My education was the sticking point in whatever the decision was. Because I was the youngest in my class, 14, and a July birthday, I was taking my intermediate certificate younger than most. In Ireland, you could leave school after this exam if you wanted to or alternatively go on for another two years and take your leaving certificate. I wanted to get my leaving cert but at the same time was desperate to become a footballer as quickly as I could. The dilemma was that if I stayed in Ireland and completed a further two years of education, I would miss out on all the coaching and the opportunity to be an apprentice with Luton or Chelsea. However, if I went to England I would still only be 15 years old and not old enough to go to school part-time. What to do was the question?

Luton came up with a suggestion. They would help my parents relocate to Luton, initially putting me up in digs. They'd also place me in a local school, where I would be educated full-time but attend youth team training sessions and be involved closely in all club events and coaching sessions. Once that first year had passed and I was sixteen, I would then become a fully-fledged apprentice but still go to school two days a week. In this way I would be getting the best of both worlds, firstly maintaining my education and secondly learning the professional game. This idea was a winner for all concerned but what about Chelsea?

Chelsea had told my parents that whatever Luton Town offered, they would be better and really stressed to my parents their keenness to sign me. I had done a terrific job when I was over there and was really impressed. I had enjoyed every minute of it but something was drawing me towards Luton. I think it was the big London thing that put me off. I made up my mind, that Luton was the club for me, worked it all out with my parents, and began to prepare myself for the challenge. Dad finally negotiated a three-year contract, which was broken down into one year schoolboy, one year apprentice, and one year professional. But first I had to make sure I passed my exams, otherwise it was all off. Did I need any more of an incentive?

Before my exams, another visit to Luton was organised. This time it was during an English holiday period, which meant I got to train and play against kids of my own age. No more of the big-time first-team stuff. I was joined by a few of my teammates from Dublin, Bobby Hogan, Paul Mulvaney, and John Clarke. We were picked up from the airport and after a 45-minute drive dropped off at our digs on Shaftsbury Rd Luton, where we were to stay with a lady by the name of Mrs Haughney. The house was a small terraced house in typical Coronation Street style. I later learned that these houses were built before the war and were home to quite affluent people at the time. However in recent years, the town had spread, people had moved to newer and bigger homes and there had been a decline in prices in the area. New immigrants from Asian countries like Pakistan and Bangladesh settled in the area and turned it into a mini Asia. It was all quite a culture shock for us Irish kids but added to the excitement. After knocking for about 5 minutes, there was still no sign of anyone home. The evening was drawing in and we began to wonder whether we'd been dropped at the right digs. The club was only 5 minutes walk away, so we decided to walk down there to see if anyone was about. As darkness fell we found the club deserted. Worry was beginning to set in. We didn't have any contact numbers apart from the address we were dropped off at and here we were with our bags in what seemed a different continent never mind a different country. After a lot of discussion between us we decided to walk back to the digs and try again, I mean maybe the lady was simply out, or maybe it was the next-door address we should have been knocking at? 'Knock, Knock' footsteps drew closer to the door. The door creaked open and there stood a thinly-haired, middle-aged man in a bathrobe. "We're looking for Mrs Haughney?" we asked. "We came by earlier but no one was home" "Yeah yeah come in, I was in the bath earlier, heard the knock but decided to stay in the bath," Des Haughney said. Des was Mrs. Haughneys son and had just come back from a training run. Des was a pretty successful long-distance runner at the time and was too tired to talk to us a lot. I remember thinking at the time how rude this seemed. We had just traveled across from Ireland and been dropped off at the door and when he heard the door he ignored it! The thing was though that Mrs Haughney had kids staying there all the time and although this was a special week for us, for him it was just another load of kids staying at his Mums house!

It was a total contrast when Mrs Haughney arrived home. She was a wonderful old Irish lady with a personality made up of genuine kindness. Her husband had died many years before and to keep some money coming in and also to have some company she looked after the football club players. One of Luton's star players Mal Donaghy had stayed with her for a long period before he eventually got married and she was exactly what a digs lady should be. Whilst I have mentioned Mal I may as well give you a bit of background. Mal was I think Northern Ireland's most capped player and had a terrific career with Luton Town. At the end of his career, he was signed by Manchester United's Alex Ferguson and had a successful period there before finishing off at Chelsea under Glen Hoddle. Mal was a true professional and a lovely guy, a chip off Mrs Haughney's block.

This week's time at Luton proved to be a more serious week. The training was quite intensive as I was competing against my peers and the touchy-feely feeling that I had experienced on previous visits to England had certainly passed. It was now about being the best and impressing the coaches. Some trial matches were held and the lads put in our best efforts. For me, it was slightly different because I knew that I was already signing for Luton, which added a little bit of confidence, whereas the other lads were still on trial. However, this did make me feel that I had to perform and justify my position which added a bit of pressure. After the week was through I learned that John Clarke was the only boy that Luton was interested in but John had also had trials with Manchester City and he opted for them instead. Unfortunately, Bobby and Paul weren't signed, which left me on my own as the sole Irish representative.

GREAVES AND O'LEARY

At some stage during the 1983/84 season, I achieved the accolade of being voted schoolboy player of the month for Ireland. This award apart from being a huge thrill meant that I was invited to attend a weekend soccer-coaching clinic in Dublin, hosted by David O'Leary and Jimmy Greaves. The idea was for 22 schoolboy players to be selected from around Ireland to take part in the course. It was a high-profile event due to the attention paid to Jimmy Greaves and David O'Leary, who were high-profile stars at the time. Jimmy Greaves was considered one of the all-time great centre forwards and was now a major television celebrity in England, whilst David O'Leary was at the height of his playing career with Arsenal football club and Ireland. We all met up at a lovely hotel south of Dublin, where we stayed over the weekend period. I roomed with my Ireland teammate David Walsh who was a Cork lad and apart from not being able to understand his Cork accent we got on great and had a terrific time.

On the first day, we all put on our supplied training kits and made our way out to the front of the hotel. A photo session had been arranged. After a group introduction to David and Jimmy, we all had individual photos taken with the two of them. This was followed by some group shots. When my turn came to have my photo taken with them, I had to crouch down 'on my hunkers' as we said in Dublin, with Jimmy on one side and David O'Leary on the other. I was so nervous that I couldn't smile due to my top lip twitching uncontrollably and though I tried desperately to stop it happening, it just kept bouncing up and down. Why I felt so nervous I don't really know, because both Jimmy and David were very relaxed down to earth people who were making a good laugh out of it all. Once the photos had been taken, my lip returned to its stable state and finally, I gained control of my body.

The training that took place was very light-hearted and good fun and Jimmy Greaves was a fantastic character who had everyone in stitches with his wisecracks. Something else that always stuck in my head was when he told us that he could never juggle the ball. Here was one of the world's greatest goal-scorers saying that he couldn't do a basic skill. However, what he did say was that "juggling the ball never put the ball in the back of the net" Now there's something to think about!

David O'Leary was like the straight man for Jimmy. In little games that we'd play He'd always try to get nutmegs and he always had to do the warm-ups, cause Greavsie comically would say "Warm-ups bore me, David can do that" David was a genuinely nice guy, and both Jimmy and he were only always interested in us kids and not the officials and press who hung around wherever you turned, two special guys.

On the last day, a match was held between Jimmy's team and David's team. Our players were split into two groups and I was placed on Jimmy's team. We played in a bowl-shaped playing field at UCD University in south Dublin. The press and football officials were invited to attend and view the players on show. A fair crowd turned up on the day and before the game began, Jimmy huddled our team together in the middle of the pitch to discuss tactics. As we sat on the grass, Jimmy asked, "Right, who wants to take penalties?" As no one put their hand up, I slowly raised mine "Okay Aaron you're the penalty taker, right who wants to take free kicks?" Once again I solely raised my hand "Okay Aaron you're on for free kicks as well, and while we're at it we might as well make you Captain". A shy lot of us Irish kids!

The game went well and afterward as the press and officials swarmed Greaves and O'Leary I can still see the frustration on the face of Greaves who really just wanted to be left alone to say cheerio to us lads, which he managed to do so despite the hangers-on attention. David wished me well on my impending trip to Luton "There is a good club and you'll get plenty of opportunity there" he said. I was looking forward to it! I met David on a few occasions in later years and he always recognised me and in his well-mannered way asked me how I was getting on. Unfortunately, I never got to see Jimmy Greaves again but was thankful for the experience.

LUTON HERE WE COME

My school exams crept up on me quicker than expected. The importance of them wasn't lost on me. I understood that education was vital should anything go wrong in my soccer career. My two brothers Graham and Derek were both hard-working students, who had performed well on all their exams, going on after school to further education. They always stressed the importance of good results and this gave me a good attitude towards education. School was never a place that I wanted to be. There wasn't any buzz to it and I can't recall a day during all my school years that I couldn't wait for that school bell to ring for the end of the day. However, I knew I had a job to do and I would complete it. I studied reasonably hard coming up to the exams, cramming a lot of information in at the last minute. Math's was a real concern, I just couldn't get to grips with algebra. One of the teachers was providing extra tuition in her own time, which you had to pay for and I desperately signed up. It worked and Math's from then on was a breeze. There is a lot to be said for one-to-one tuition. The exams finished with me passing all subjects bar one 'Irish language', but Hey let's face it, did that matter?

Aaron Tighe

With my exams successfully out of the way, our thoughts turned back to my impending future as a footballer with Luton Town in England. It was the summer of 1984 and I was about to turn 15 years old. Luton had comfortably avoided relegation during the 83/84 season and was now established in the top flight. I was looking forward to the challenge that lay ahead. A small family going away/birthday party was arranged. Eddie Corcoran the Luton scout came along, along with some friends. The time had arrived to travel. My schoolboy dreams of becoming a professional were becoming a reality.

My parents traveled with me, as they were tying up some loose ends in England, as well as seeing me make the transition smoothly. We stayed at a small guesthouse called the 'Grange' in a suburb of Luton called Leagrave. Another new arrival at the club was also staying there by the name of Ashley Grimes. This was the man who I had seen score the cracker against Argentina in Dublin, the Man Utd guy, the guy who had been one of my Man Utd heroes, the guy who had been on posters on my wall!

I had previously met Ashley in a dark lane that runs alongside Dalymount Park in Dublin. We had been to watch a testimonial match for Don Givens and Ashley had been playing. After the game, I waited with my mate outside the player's entrance and as Ashley exited, he ran to avoid the crowd of autograph hunters that had gathered in the narrow dark alleyway. Unfortunately for him, we ran as well eventually slowing him down enough to get him to sign our autograph books, which took pride of place ahead of my Banbury Utd autographs.

Well, here we were sitting in the bar area of the Grange Hotel, chatting to Ashley. I was still very shy and my Mum and Dad were doing all the talking, particularly my Mum. Ashley sat in what I would soon learn was the 'footballer relaxing look' with his right foot resting on his left knee, a glass and bottle of Perrier water sitting on the table in front of him. Ashley had just joined the club from Coventry City and had begun pre-season training hence the Perrier water.

Ashley was a funny mad character and would sometimes look at you with the most distrusting look I have ever seen like you were about to steal a million dollars from him, but at the same time a little grin would appear and then you'd realise he was messing. I can remember on one occasion walking through Luton's Arndale indoor shopping centre and on seeing Ashley approach, I said "Hi Ash" as you do. He glanced at me and then proceeded to walk straight by me without a word and not even a nod of the head, nothing. At the time I thought' you rude so and so' but that was his way of taking the micky.

Similarly, I remember us sitting around the dressing room one day when Ashley walked out of the medical room with just a towel wrapped around his waist and stopped suddenly in the middle of the room. As we watched, he stared for a few seconds at the floor and suddenly lashed out with his foot at a hanger that was lying innocently on the dressing room carpet "Get out of my 'expletive' way" he yelled before walking on and sitting down without a flicker of humour on his face and without raising his eyes to anyone, as we all giggled away at his manic humour.

I ended up as Ashley's apprentice for a year and he was great with me. One of my jobs was to make sure I brought his kit and boots to the training ground in the morning and on one occasion when he arrived; he discovered that his apprentice Aaron Tighe had completely forgotten. Without a sour word, he drove me back to the club to get the kit to help me out and not get me into trouble. Needless to say, I never forget anyone's kit again.

It was soon time for me to start training and for Mum and Dad to return home to Dublin. Although they were planning to return to live, it would take a few months for anything to happen. Temporary digs were arranged with a nice old lady called Olive, who was a friend of Mrs Haughney and lived on the same road.

Aaron Tighe

The day arrived when Mum and Dad said goodbye and as Mum walked out to the car, I heard her crying. It was then that I realised that for the first time in my life, I really was on my own. As I lay in bed that night, I feared that I would miss home terribly and that I would hate it in Luton, so I imagined lying in my own bed at home just in case. During the next couple of weeks, I joined in training with the apprentices and trialists. David Coates had been assigned as the new youth team coach. It was actually a demotion from being first-team coach but what a blessing for us kids as his knowledge and enthusiasm for the game was inexhaustible. Homesickness never took hold thank God and soon I was into a routine.

This was the time of the dreaded pre-season training when physical fitness made up the main bulk of the work. I had been training hard in Dublin with my brother Derek and was prepared for the onslaught. As well as Ashley Luton had signed Vince Hilaire. Vince as a youngster was one of England's brightest prospects and I remembered him as one of the players who performed on the English FA coaching videos. One day we were doing track running on a cinder oval at the training ground and poor old Vince couldn't stop throwing up at the end, the funny thing was he just shrugged it off like it was just one of those things. A few of the players got to know me that day as I held my own in the dreaded 12-minute run and 400' s. I was still only 15 years old and weighed a mere 10 stone. In fact, the manager David Pleat was concerned about my weight and kept saying that I needed to get stronger.

Another player who was training at the time was the former England Captain Gerry Francis. He was at the end of his career and was probably making that transition between finishing playing and moving on to something else. On one occasion a practice match was held between the first team and the reserves and David Pleat called out for me to join in the game for the reserves. So there I was playing against 'Gerry Francis', another guy who I used to have on my football cards back in Banbury. Whilst training at Luton He'd wear some plastic pants, which looked like a big plastic nappy, obviously helping him to sweat and shed a few pounds. This was a common sight for the older bigger players who had put on a few extra pounds over the close season. I don't think he stayed too long at Luton but it was great to play and train with him anyhow.

Gerry Francis wasn't the only star to pass through that summer. During the close season, David Pleat who was highly regarded as a shrewd man in the transfer market had just sold England International Paul Walsh to Liverpool for a club record fee of 700,000 pounds and hence had some money to spend whilst also searching for some experienced players to help strengthen his squad. Chelsea's giant defender Mickey Droy and the old Derby defender Colin Todd were also former picture card heroes of mine who passed through Luton at this time. It was an awesome experience for a shy kid like me to be involved with people of their stature and thinking back was a little overwhelming.

Another nice surprise during those few weeks was when my brother Derek paid me a surprise visit for a couple of days. Derek came down and watched us train and it was great to have him there. After a couple of days, I could still clearly see him saying goodbye outside the entrance to the football ground as he headed off to visit our old hometown of Banbury, reminding me that I was staying here for good and things were never going to be the same!

For young players who leave home to go to football clubs, particularly from another country, it is a big step in their young lives from being within the family unit, you are thrust out into the big and foreign world on your own. You have independence and are only bound by the rules of work but at the same time that feeling of safety that you get from being at home is taken from under you and you can feel like you on the wire without a net. I have seen numerous cases where homesickness got to young players and the feeling became so overwhelming that they couldn't concentrate on their job, football, eventually packing in and heading back to that safe place called home. In my case, I truly felt that becoming a professional footballer was my destiny. I don't mean that in an arrogant way, as I was a very nervous person on the surface but deep inside I really believed it was meant to be. My success to date told me that I just seemed to be on the right path, heading in the exact direction that I should be, and as long as I worked hard it would happen.

My couple of weeks with Olive came to an end as digs had been arranged for me with a young family, who lived on the outskirts of Luton about 20 minutes drive from the ground, in an area called Warden Hills. The houses were modern and newly built and I very quickly settled in. Brian and Cathy Meatyard had two kids, Kerry who was 11 years old, and Kevin who was nine. They also had a lovely big Labrador-type dog called Barney who I'd take running up the hills, getting him totally filthy before returning him home safely. They were wonderful hosts and I was their first lodger. The reason I stayed there was the close proximity of the catholic school that I was enrolled in for the forthcoming school year. Brian was involved in the education area and had been instrumental in setting up my schooling with the club. I was only fifteen and by English law had to remain in full-time education until the age of 16. The important thing from a football sense was that I would be involved with the Luton youth team every week and the experience would be invaluable.

School got underway and I entered into it with a mature attitude knowing that it was important to do well and build on what turned out to be a successful intermediate exam in Dublin. However, my real focus was my career as a professional footballer and performing the best I could at all times. My first few games for the Luton youth team were uneventful and just like when I made the transition from Tymon Bawn to Stella Maris I found the pace difficult and the physical element hard to adjust to. At this stage, I was 15 years old playing in an under 17/18 youth league and against

England's best youth players, so the jump was greater but once again after a while I settled down and began to play well.

Our coach David Coates who had previously been the 1st team coach as I mentioned earlier had been switched to youth team coach. David was a terrific guy and one of the most enthusiastic football coaches I have met. During the season we would gather on a Wednesday night for training at Kenilworth Road, Luton's ground. Once changed in the dressing room we'd wait for 'Coatsy' as we called him to come and fetch us to start training. However, David was a football romantic and a person who, should you get him talking about football, would get carried away and talk about it forever. On some occasions, we'd sit in the dressing room listening to his stories of the two headers he scored against Liverpool at Anfield, or similar tales of heroism on his part when he was a player. With hardly any time left for training, he'd say, "Well I suppose we'd better go out and have a five a side or something". A little reluctantly we'd leave the dressing room and the great tales of his football past.

Coatsy had amazing football knowledge and a photographic memory of football statistics and events. Years after I had finished playing I met David at a football match and it was like meeting an old friend. We talked about the team and he could recall games and goalscorers for virtually every match that we played, telling me in his excited larger-than-life way.

The training was held on the football club's tarmac car park and Coatsy gave me my first lessons on how to play 'good football'. That's a term that you hear lots of people say, like "They're a footballing team" etc. All it means is that you play the game skillfully and thoughtfully. For example instead of a team just booting the ball as far they can in the direction of the goal, they pass the ball and move and look for the next pass, etc creating a smooth interaction between players. That's how Luton played and also teams like West Ham, Tottenham and Liverpool. Fortunately,

Aaron Tighe

I had developed as what's termed a 'ball player', suited to that style of football. The thing was, our youth team was full of good footballers and before long we were the league leaders despite the majority of us being a year underage. Coatsy would also coach us before games with things like set pieces and throw-ins. A great favourite with managers and players to this day is the 'throw down the line'. "What's that" Coatsy would say if someone threw the ball aimlessly down the line, or high to someone's head or chest. "We've gained possession; let's not just give it back to them. Throw it to feet, so he can control it". Coatsy had worked out a throw-in that had worked successfully in the first team with Brian Stein and Paul Walsh, whereby the players line up one in front of the other on an angle facing the thrower. They would both begin to move down the line but the furthest player would check back inside and the thrower was left with a simple throw to this player's feet, the first player having created a space by his continued run down the line. Coatsy got us to practice it until we had it to perfection and from that point on we never gave away a throw-in, in fact, we enhanced it so that we turned it into a goalscoring opportunity around the box, a simple thing but very effective.

The Youth team included four schoolboy internationals. There was me from the Republic of Ireland, Richard Harvey a left-back for England, Duncan Berry a centre-back for England, and Paul Lewis from Wales. There were also some very talented lads like left-winger Kingsley Black, defender Marvin Johnson, midfielder/centre-back Ian Scott, and centre-forward Sean Farrell. We were also joined by apprentices Gary Cobb a midfielder, Ricky Mc Evoy that outstanding Irish schoolboy international I had watched play in Dublin and centre-forward David Oldfield. Local lads such as center-forward Gary Williams, defender Jonathon Bone, and midfielder Sandor Gaylog also did well for us that season. When you talk about outstanding teams this was one and under the watchful and excited eye of David Coa, nothing could stop us winning the league.

Despite being a young team we were carving teams up with fast-flowing passing football. On one occasion at home, we were up against Tottenham. The game was played at our home pitch, a lovely playing surface at a place called Talbots in Houghton Regis, a suburb of Luton. I had a terrific battle in midfield against a Tottenham lad by the name of Vinnie Samways who later went on to have a very successful career at Spurs. At some stage in the game, we noticed David Pleat walking towards the pitch with the rest of the first team. The game kicked off at 11 o'clock and the boss had brought them down to watch us before they played their first division match in the afternoon at 3. Mr. Pleat told them that they should watch us play as we played football the way it should be played, a nice compliment from the Boss!

David Pleat had a way of making kids feel very important, his style of management was such that with just a few words he could make a kid feel a million dollars. After a particular first team game, I was invited in to see the physio John Sheridan as I had a knock or something. The game had only just finished, so as I entered the Home team dressing room, I was confronted By Mr. Pleat who was standing just inside the door with the Chairman of the club David Evans. "Mr. Chairman," Pleat said " This is aaarun Tighe", he never could pronounce my name right, "one of our brightest prospects". With just those few words I felt like I could take on the world. I would learn years later that he could in as many words also send you in the other direction with regard to confidence but more of that later.

THE GREATEST TEAM

One of the finest football displays that I have seen wasn't Brazil's team of 1982 or Manchester United's many glorious teams but a game we played against Oxford's youth team in 1985. We were sitting at the top of the league at the time and Oxford were our closest rivals in second. The game was played at Oxford's training ground and I recall there being a good build-up to the game in the precluding days, as it was important for both teams to win to maintain the title challenge. Before the game, as I was warming up on the pitch, I noticed a definite larking about attitude by some of our players which didn't sit well with me. This was an important game for us and I felt that if they carried the same attitude into the match we may struggle. Fortunately, I couldn't have been more wrong.

As well as the excitement of the game another edge was added when David Pleat turned up to watch the game and remained in his car behind one of the goals throughout the whole game, a little odd but it was good for him to be there. To cut a long story short by halftime we were winning four nil, which was great, but the way we did it was awesome. I had never and would never play again in a team, which clicked so well and played such fantastic pacey pass and move football. We ran an absolute riot against the Oxford lads and they really didn't know whether they were coming or going. At half time in the dressing room as I watched David Coates I could see in his eyes that he was shell-shocked by what he had just seen "Lads, in all my years as a footballer and a coach, I have never seen such an exhibition of football" he said as if in a daze. The thing was I knew exactly what he was saying. Whenever you received the ball there were teammates supporting you from all over the place and the ball just kept pinging its way around in flowing one-touch and two-touch football. We went out for the second half not really knowing what to expect. Although we never reached the peaks of football brilliance of the first half, we scored a further 9 goals as Oxford simply collapsed under the onslaught. I along with Gary Cobb and Sean Farrell grabbed hat tricks and the final result ended 13 - 1. If I remember rightly the result made headlines in all of the local papers and even in some national ones. Not a bad youth team!

After our games, we'd get on the coach and head back down to Kenilworth Road, usually with enough time to grab a bag of chips in the local chippy before going to watch the first team play against whomever. These games although not quite the same as watching Man Utd play Barcelona, were exciting events as Luton was up against Arsenal and Man Utd's week in and week out. Pleat in the run-up to Christmas had strengthened the team with some shrewd purchases and over the second half of the 84/85 season was the second-best-performing team in the league. Pleat had signed former England centre-half Steve Foster from Aston Villa (the guy with the headband), Welsh international midfielder Peter Nicholas, the best slide tackler I have ever seen, David Preece a left-sided midfielder with terrific passing capabilities, and big centre-forward Mick Harford who would later become an England international with Luton. These players combined with Luton's other internationals Brian Stein, Ricky Hill, and Mal Donaghy formed an excellent footballing team, that played exciting passing football with a solid spine right down the middle. Things were looking up for Luton but it would be tough to break through as a youngster, However, that seemed a long way away for me at this stage, plenty of time to develop I thought to myself.

To this day I still think of myself as a little kid at this stage of my career and it's funny because as a coach in recent years, I have looked after the same age group at a school of excellence level and the guys seem anything but kids just through sheer size let alone anything else. It's easy to forget that at the ages of 15,16,17, they are still kids even though they may look like grown-ups. At the same time, it's important I feel to let them know that they are physically grown up enough at the age of 16,17 to compete against adults or senior players and all they need is that belief to do so. Certainly, at these ages in my career, I was always spoken of as a prospect and that bred the mindset that I was still a kid and first-team football was years away. On learning my lesson I have tried to pass on the message to new professionals that if you are good enough you can be playing regular first-team football at seventeen and to go for that, why settle for less, speak to your coach and find out what you need to do to get there. I was throughout my playing career too respectful towards coaches and managers to the point where I was scared to ask for advice for fear of what they'd say. Some guys took the opposite path and went on to have fruitful careers. I think the moral is to review your performance regularly with the coach and don't wait for them to speak to you, you go to them.

My first season as a Luton Town player drew to a close in May of 1985. Under the watchful eye of David Coates, we performed amazing things and I learned how to play as a professional rather than a kid. My positional sense on the pitch was excellent due to Coatsy and along with a talented bunch of players, we had really kicked some ass. The finale of the season was a presentation of the league trophy before a first-team game at a packed Kenilworth road. Dressed in our strips we carried the trophy aloft on a lap of honour to rapturous applause. This was a great achievement for a small club like Luton and the club wanted the fans to know that they had proven, they were bringing kids to the club who were a match for anyone. My football career was still right on track and fate would get me to the very top. I could feel it deep down in my heart.

With the end of the season came the selection of players as apprentices, that is full-time 16-year-olds, who whilst training would carry out various tasks which would supposedly turn them into men and teach them discipline and the like. Some of us were in for a shock with just how hard this period would be and not all would make it through the season.

The club selected 9 boys, Firstly there was me the only Irishman, followed by Richard Harvey an English international full-back and by far the strongest among us, thirdly there was Duncan Berry another English international, fourth there was Paul Lewis of Wales, fifth there was Ian Scott our skillful local midfielder, sixth there was John Kennedy from Wales, Seventh there was local defender Marvin Johnson with his big afro (great looking at those old photos), eighth came a welsh lad by the name of Matthew Bowden and last but not least was our goal scoring machine Sean Farrell, who had only been selected at the last minute.

This was an enthralling story, Sean was an extremely quiet lad who said boo to a goose but on the field, he had this knack of being in the right place at the right time to score goals. During the season on a Wednesday night training Coatsie would continually get us to form a circle around Sean striking balls into him, Sean was tasked with controlling the ball quickly and laying it off. Coats ie saw the potential goal-scoring attributes but recognised that his touch had to improve hence the practice. Come selection time David Pleat told Coatsie that he didn't feel Sean was a good enough 'footballer' and that he didn't feel he would make it. Coatsie argued "But David, he keeps scoring goals, you can't ignore that". Coatsie made a bet with Pleat, stating that if he scored in the last game of the season (or close to it if that wasn't the exact match) then Pleat would take him on. Of course, Sean without knowing the importance of the game managed to score, and when Coates made the phone call to Pleat after the game Pleat asked, "Well who scored?" "Who do you think?" replied Coates "ok he's on board" acknowledged Pleat. That was that, Sean had made it and deservedly so. It can be a fine line between making it and not, but Sean had proven himself time and time again and this put him in the position of that last match. Fortunately, he hadn't blown it.

Aaron Tighe

Top left, in the back garden of Bretch Hill Banbury in my Everton kit where I'd kick the ball against our big blue gate for hours at end dreaming of being a footballer. Top right with my local team Tymon Bawn in Dublin with my bearded Dad top left and me bottom row 2nd from left.

Top, competing in the national Coca-Cola skills competition where I achieved the highest points score in Ireland. At the age of 11 I was juggling over 2000. Below with top Dublin team Stella Maris, the Man Utd of schoolboy football.

1983 with my Dublin national champion teammates and thrilled to bits holding the Kennedy Cup as captain. Meeting and working with the legends Jimmy Greaves and David O'Leary.

Above, My 1st International experience in 1983 v Wales. Left-bottom, at the airport about to travel to England to trial with top-flight Luton Town, followed by Chelsea. Right-bottom, with my cousin John watching the 1983 Man Utd team arrive at Wembley for the FA Cup Final.

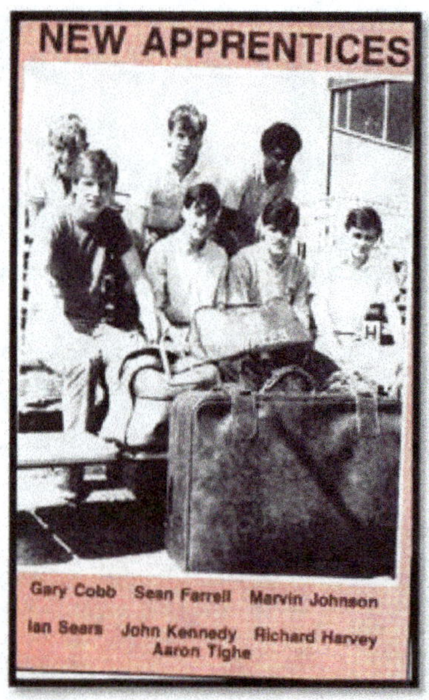

Top - A working life begins and boy did we work hard. My fellow apprentices 1985. Below photo that was used to promote how successful our club was in attracting the best youth players. Our international youth players with caps. From left to right Ricky McEvoy. Paul Lewis, Mick Obrien, myself, Marcus Tuite, Neil Poutch, Paul Gray, Richard Harvey, Ian Scott.

Luton Town squad 1985. I'm front row 5th left

Youth Champs 1985 and Youth Cup winners 1988

1st team 1989, I'm top row 2nd from left between mates Jason Reece and Mick Obrien.

Aaron Tighe

●Great prospect: Aaron Tighe.

Aaron aiming ahead for big future

Born in Dublin, Aaron Tighe is one of the brightest young prospects in the Town's reserves and has produced several fine performances in the Sunday Mirror Combination team.

A skilful, physically strong left-sided player, Aaron has won the praise of many observers for his attacking skills.

Aaron has an eye for goal as well and his combination of midfield skill and power makes him an outstanding prospect in a department where the Town are already very strong.

Aged 19 this year, he will be fighting to break through to the senior squad and follow in the successful footsteps of Kingsley Black who has won several first team appearances this season.

● Big future: Aaron Tighe.

Aaron Tighe provided a composed senior debut when he was selected for the Zenith Data Cup tie at Crystal Palace. He is pictured in action during that game.

GLORIOUS HOLLAND

At the end of every season, the club participated in a number of top-class youth and under-21 tournaments in Holland. The first one that I played in was the prestigious 1985 Feynoord under 21 tournament in Rotterdam. I had just completed my first year with the club and still aged 15, was excited by the prospect of playing against foreign opposition. On arrival in Holland, we were driven by coach to our accommodation and out in a sticks chalet-style complex, the ideal place to take a young football team, particularly if you want to take the competition seriously. The nearest town was miles away making nighttime excursions very difficult for those easily led astray.

The competition matches were played in the magnificent Feynoord stadium in Rotterdam. The first day that we pulled up to the stadium I was in awe at the sheer size of the structure. Inside, we had the pleasure of occupying the home team dressing room, a facility that you could almost play a five a side in, at least that's what it seemed like compared to Luton's dressing rooms. On the pitch, you got a little tingle of excitement by just being there, with towering stands all around us and beautiful lush green grass, perfect for a passing game.

Aaron Tighe

Despite my excitement, I was bitterly disappointed to be left out of the opening game against the mighty Ajax of Amsterdam. In hindsight, it turned out to be a blessing but at the time I couldn't believe it when the coach in charge, reserve manager John Moore selected a more senior centre-forward David Old field in the left midfield position. John had decided to play a sweeper at the back, to try and counter the way the opposition were expected to play. As I sat on the bench admiring the skills of the Dutch lads, the sweeper system began to wilt. At half-time John admitted that things weren't going to plan "we haven't got a clue what we're doing out there and neither do they" said John. The team reverted to a more British 4 - 4 - 2 formation, but the damage was done and Ajax won easily.

For the next game, I was elected to play left midfield in the more accustomed four in midfield. Although it wasn't my favourite position, I was delighted to get a chance and was equally determined to prove my place. from that game on we never looked back, reaching a crunch semifinal with the French Champions Bordeaux. With our game plan of everybody behind the ball and breaking forward quickly when we had the opportunity, we held Bordeaux at bay. Late in the game left-back Richard Harvey hit a long-range effort, which deflected, into the net and the Jubilant Luton were through to the final. The only disappointment was that fellow Dublin Midfielder Ricky Mc Evoy had received a suspected broken foot and was rushed to hospital, a lesson to us all, to never strike through a ball in a 50 - 50 situation. The Bordeaux player went in with his studs showing, leaving the talented Ricky in a lot of pain.

In recent years I have used the following story in Sales seminars to show an example of how powerful teamwork can be when carried out with commitment. The team that we were up against in the final was the team that had comfortably beaten us in the opening game, Ajax! Ajax was undoubtedly a team of more skillful players, players blessed with superb technique, so the challenge that stood before us was a tough one, however, we had come through victorious against some excellent competition and were confident that we could hold our own.

As we prepared for the game, the morale of the team was sky high, the team spirit was powerful, and everybody knew exactly what their role was in the team. We also knew the role of every other player in the team and hence could offer encouragement or rollickings if need be, to make sure everyone did what they were there to do. The tactics were simple, fall back to 40 yards from our goal when not in position and compress the Ajax attacking third. As soon as we won the ball, we were to play the ball to centre-forward Mark North's feet and break quickly. It was simple but hugely effective. Everyone knew their specific job.

As expected Ajax was superior in possession of the lush green grass, pressing us back. This was the era of Ajax's Van Basten's and Gullits, very talented young players. Defending like our lives depended on it; we'd eventually win the ball and break. Marc North, one of our over-age players, who went on to win player of the tournament, used his pace to score some terrific goals. The final result ended in an emphatic 4 - 2 win for us, a truly amazing turnaround from the match played only a few days earlier. I recall threading through a long pass for the final goal and watching Marc score as my legs cramped up from tiredness. However the joy of winning the tournament made all the pain go away and as the team along with coach John Moore and Chief Scout Ron Howard picked up the trophy, my emotions got the better of me and the tears of pride began to flow. That night we celebrated in Rotterdam town centre and even Ricky Mc Evoy with a plastercast around his left foot, danced in the street. What a team and what a difference committed teamwork makes!

Our trips to Holland over the following two years, under the leadership of reserve team manager Jimmy Ryan and youth coach John Faulkener, saw us reach similar heights with fantastic teams and team spirit. During this period we won the Den Hagg international club tournament in both years as well as challenging in other tournaments. As more experienced players, the victories weren't quite as sweet as the Feyenoord occasion but even so, the Dutch tournaments bring back great memories of terrific teamwork and camaraderie, a beautiful feeling that only comes from a lot of people pulling together to achieve success.

The Dutch excursions are memorable also for other reasons not related directly to football. As older players, every year we would take part in the Blauw Wit tournament in Amsterdam. This tournament would prove to be a disaster on the football field every year but a huge success off it. The trip was purely used as a release for the players, a way to let off steam after a long hard season. Unlike the Feyenoord or Den Haag tournaments, where we'd be under close surveillance in a hotel or sports complex, during this tournament we'd stay in digs for the long weekend. Me and fellow midfielder Ian Scott were always paired up in the digs and we'd have a ball. For two years running, we stayed with a fantastic couple on the outskirts of the beautiful city of Amsterdam. Barry, who was about 6 foot 5 and Corinne laid up some beds in their loft conversion and looked after us like we were family. Barry a butcher and shop owner obviously had no shortage of money and took us out to dine in some of the finest restaurants in Amsterdam. Afterward, we'd meet up with the rest of the lads and hit the town, rolling home at four or five in the morning, resisting Barry's wishes to stay out longer. Me and Scotty got on famously and would embark on long conversations about football, life in general, and of course being the age we were, girls! During one evening in an Amsterdam nightclub, two gorgeous girls approached us and asked us to dance. Thinking we were in luck, we headed for the dance floor only for the girls to vanish after 10 minutes or so. As we stood at the bar wondering what happened, a confused Barry approached "Vere ar the girls?" asked Barry "Don't know" replied

Scotty "They disappeared" but I paid them to stay with you for the night!" exclaimed Barry!

As the lads appeared bleary-eyed and barely sober in the dressing room every morning, the coaches would turn a blind eye. One of the funniest incidents I recall was Gary Cobb, our right-side midfielder heading a ball only to take about five minutes to get up from the ground afterward, or my good friend Neil Poutch, normally a teetotaler, projectile vomiting as he sat on the bench as a substitute, I mean, some sub he was going to be.

As well as bars and clubs the red light district of Amsterdam certainly kept a few of the lads entertained. One of the lads achieved the amazing task of entering and leaving the same establishment twice within five minutes. Keeping names out of it, another player who had lost his digs address managed to sleep underneath a stand at the football ground, as it was the only address that he knew to tell the taxi driver at five in the morning. The amazing thing was that despite all the social activities that were going on we still managed to compete in two or three matches a day over the course of the weekend, albeit badly.

APPRENTISHIP
1985/86

With my sixteenth birthday only weeks away, my adult life was about to begin. Although it had been arranged that I would still go to school two days a week to complete certain 'O' level studies, this was considered the break away from school to a working life. A 'working life', can you really consider professional football to be working? Well actually yes it is, bloody hard work at that, full-on physical and mental pressure day after day as you competed to impress the coaches. It may not have been 9 to 5 but mentally it was 24/7.

By this time I was living back with my parents in a small bungalow in Repton Close Luton. They had kept the family house in Ireland where my 20-year-old brother Derek would remain. Graham my eldest brother had long since flown the nest and was now working and living in a small town north of Dublin called Drogheda. The family had broken up and Mum and Dad felt it was important to come to England to support me. It was always going to be a short-term thing but was an amazing step for them to take. Dad got a job with the local giant Vauxhall and the club played their part in helping them to relocate and putting them in touch with the best people.

Aaron Tighe

Our first week at the club as apprentices was what I had expected ' hard work'. The only surprise was that our heroic coach of the season before 'David Coates' had moved on and an ex-Luton and Leeds centre-half John Faulkener was taking over. None of us lads ever found out why Coatsie had bitten the bullet but the fact was that he was gone and we had to get on with it and the reserve team coach at Luton, Trevor Hartley, stepped up to 1st team coach. Trevor had been a professional with West Ham. He was a little fella but packed a punch and was someone who drove the player's performance very hard. Our new coach John Faulkener was still on holiday for a week when we started training and I overheard one of the coaching staff say whilst shaking his head "That's not a good start, fancy not wanting to be with the lads during the first week of training" ouch, even coaches were competitive.

I'd go on to see a not-so-nice competitive streak side of some players over the years, like new players being introduced in the dressing room and players completely turning away when introduced, basically setting their stall out if they saw the player as competition and making them as unwelcome as possible. Players at all levels also could be seen completely "blanking" as it was called by other players to once again let them know no love was lost when you're fighting for your living.

Both Trevor and reserve coach John Moor e put us through our paces in the first week. On day 1 we were allocated our jobs and players to look after. I was to look after the international stars Ashley Grimes and Ricky Hill. This involved bringing their kit to and from training, cleaning their boots, making them tea, and anything else that they could think of. We were also allocated the cleaning up jobs, which were rotated weekly. These involved cleaning the home team and away team dressing rooms, cleaning the bath, shower, and toilet areas (the worst job in the world especially as some players would make it as messy as they could), looking after all the equipment, and making the big pots of tea. Have you ever made tea for 40 players? That's a big pot! Of course, these jobs were on top of training twice a day and by 5.30 when you'd leave the ground, bed was the only thing you were thinking of.

The discipline thrown out by the coaches would be comparable with the army. At the end of the day, we'd all sit in the home team dressing room awaiting ' the inspection', which was mainly carried out by the now-appointed Reserve Coach John Moore. One of the lads would knock on the coach's room door letting him know that we were finished cleaning up. John would then leave us waiting for a while before quietly entering the dressing room and seeking out areas where we hadn't done a good job. He would do things like run his fingers along the top of door frames checking for dust and look for the slightest bit of dirt on a pair of football boots hanging up in the boot room. Meanwhile, we would sit praying that we had done our job well. Then it would happen "John Kennedy (or whoever was unfortunate enough), get in here" We'd then hear the lecture about 'if you can't do a simple job here how can you hope to be a footballer. A footballer requires discipline to do the job the first time blah blah blah'. We of course then had to wait for the job to be done properly before any of us could go home. The culprit of course received some fierce stick from the lads and once the job was complete, we would have to go through the same process of knocking on the coach's room door, John leaving us waiting and then eventually coming in to inspect. This wasn't a one-off thing, it happened every day. Looking back I really don't know how John didn't laugh because it really was a farcical situation. Here was a bunch of young footballers that had to be cleaners? However, John carried out the seriousness of it all like his life depended on it and we were all scared to not impress.

FEAR

"Does surrender lead to grief, Tell me is it brave to fall Doubt can sometimes smother belief or am I just a fool"

— Aaron Tighe "Blessing in Disguise" Copyright
© 1991

I once read the autobiography of the great Pat Jennings. Pat was one of the most famous goalkeepers who had carved out a long and immensely successful career with Tottenham and Northern Ireland during the 60's and 70's from my recollection he stated in his book, in effect, that he didn't enjoy being a professional footballer due to the pressure that he was constantly under. I at this young age knew exactly where he was coming from. Call it nerves or whatever but I used to hate the trip to the training pitch and the initial getting ready for training. It was a very uncomfortable time for me. The fun and excitement of being at a professional football club had worn away big time and the pressure had set in. I felt that I had to impress but the level had just jumped a million miles upwards. On the small coach that we would all cram into on the way to training, a DJ on Radio 1 would tell a sad story every morning about some poor unfortunate soul who had lost love or had experienced a tragedy in their lives. The senior players would take the mickey and laugh and joke whilst we youngsters sat or stood wondering what drills we would be put through today. So strong were my feelings that I would hope that traffic lights would turn red as we approached, just to give us a little bit more time before the physical and mental battle began.

I suppose you have to understand that when you're kids playing out on the road or in the local park it's purely fun, there is nobody judging you, apart from your friends, but they're your friends whether you win, lose, play rubbish or play fantastic. In professional football, your teammates are also your competitors. The very best players are chosen to play in the first team, so you must be the best and that means shining more than your teammate. Every day and at every moment during training and matches, you are fighting to impress the coaches and your peers. It's tough. I read somewhere that team sports such as football, hockey, rugby, etc are the toughest sports mentally because you are competing with each other as well as against other teams at all times, in training and matches.

I realise that these feelings that I had were nerves. As time passed and I got a little older I managed to find a mental state, that coped with this better. I had gained a lot of respect from both senior players and peers and just got on with it. As the advertisement says 'just do it' and that was the attitude of mind I'd focus on, I've got to do it, so prepare yourself to do it. Those nerves never went away but I learned to live with them and to this day it has made me a much stronger person menta l ly, to the point where I have every confidence in what I do as long as I find that mental state 'prepare yourself, let's do it and be good at it.

I recall during one training session on Luton's plastic, Ray Harford the first team coach at the time, held a penalty shootout at the end of training. I watched as Richard Harvey, already a first-team player since the age of 16, prepared to take the penalty. Although it was only considered a bit of fun, the first team manager was watching. Whilst some of the lads laughed and joked about it, Richard was totally focused and comfortably scored with a confident strike into the bottom right-hand corner of the goal. I learned from watching Richard that day and always tried to copy his attitude. Stay focused.

PRE SEASON TRAINING

Pre-season would always start in the first or second week of July and boy did I hate pre-season. The first year as an apprentice had to be the toughest physical test of my life. I went into it pretty fit as I made sure that physical work was done the few weeks prior. A lot of the time this would be carried out in Ireland while I was on holiday, sometimes with my brother Derek who would join in and push me. We would run up to the hell fire Club, which is an old ruin that stands at the very peak of Dublin Mountain and can be seen from miles around by the people of Dublin. This hill was the kind that you almost had to put your hands down to keep yourself from falling backward. We'd race up the dirt track to the top which was a fair distance, sucking in the fresh mountain air and pumping our arms and legs. This was a typical training method I would use to improve my fitness. Although I never really enjoyed running, I enjoyed the challenge that it laid down and somewhere along the line, I had been told never to stop and walk, to always keep on my toes, even if it was slower than walking. For as long as I can remember when I hit a wall whilst running that voice would enter my head "Don't walk or you cheat yourself".

Aaron Tighe

This backfired on me in one particular pre-season. After a thirty-minute run around the lovely Warden Hills area of Luton, we were faced with a huge steep incline, which once completed led to a final run across an open field to the finish line and a beautiful cool drink and desperately required rest. As I approached the bottom of the hill I passed our first team midfielder David Preece (David was a left-sided midfielder and therefore a competitor) who was walking up the hill. Using this inner voice "Don't stop, keep on your toes" I struggled to the top of the hill never once dropping my pace. The problem was the hill took it out of me, the legs were shot and I just didn't have a fast finish. As I pushed towards the finish line David who had taken a nice rest walking up the hill came sprinting past me in what looked like a terrific show of determination. "Fantastic David" shouted one of the coaches "Great effort" Silently and unnoticed I finished!

On one of these typical early pre-season runs I managed to tuck in behind Irish international al Mal Donaghy and mentally told myself "If I can stick with Mal then I've done a good job". Since then often whilst running long distances I picture myself tucked in behind someone, this has become one way of driving through the pain. It's always easier to run with somebody rather than on your own.

The first time I was physically ill training (a la Vince Hilaire) was at Luton's athletics track. This is a professional athletics facility, which is based close to the M1 motorway in Luton. The track sits in a sunken oval with high embankments all around. As you approach, the knowledge of what you're about to go through gives you a sunken feeling in your stomach. Half-hearted jokes are spluttered out by the lads around you to cover the nervousness. The Gladiators approach the Coliseum! The track here was excellent quality, made of that red rubbery stuff that gives a bounce to your step, the white lines that formed the lanes looked like train tracks stretching out in front of you as a reminder of the distance that you'll be running and inside you feel competitive adrenaline, which begins to flow. May the best man win!

Trevor Hartley the first team coach on this occasion was the man dishing out the orders, instructions or whatever you wish to call them, orders if you ask me. The session started with a 12-minute run, the typical footballer's test of stamina carried out as a standard the world over. A 12-minute run sounds easy, I mean it's only 12 minutes, think about it, 12 minutes is nothing, but let me tell you it's nothing until you and 30+ other guys are trying to beat each other and run like hell to do it. The race started and as expected the pace was frantic from the beginning. You were expected to do at least 8 laps of the track and by lap 1 the lungs were burning, the legs screamed out 'Stop please stop' but pride and the will to win overcame the initial pain barrier until you slowed to a pace that was more comfortable. Even at that stage, your body nags at you to stop but if you do, you've lost, and losing was never an option.

At the end of the initial 12-minute run, we'd crouch over and eventually stand straight sucking in the air as quickly as we could before the second running session commenced, two 400 metre runs. The group was split into 10 per group. For those unaccustomed to running tracks, 400 metres is one lap of the track. Players that were on their last legs a few minutes before suddenly find a burst of energy, which from the word go enables them to sprint the first 50 metres before succumbing to a lack of oxygen to the necessary body parts. Once again I'd fight my body to beat the competition. Once again just as the legs and lungs recovered at the end of the race, you were on starter orders and off again.

It was during the second of these races that my stomach decided to fight back. Halfway around the track its control went AWOL. The funny thing was that my mind was still going "Don't stop or you're a loser" as my stomach exploded like a volcano sending bile and the remains of my small breakfast straight out of my mouth onto the grassed areas next to the track. However, my stomach was on its own in this rebellion as my legs and other parts remained under my mind's control continuing their onward painful journey towards the final bend. With my head tilted sideways I managed to projectile away from my body, thus making sure that no damage was done to my kit or those around me as my legs never stopped on their forward journey.

"Once you've been sick you still have 50% of your energy left" shouted Trevor as he lined us up for the four 200-metre runs. Then followed the four 100-metre sprints and finally the end, at least until tomorrow.

One of the apprentices Duncan Berry was a great lad. He had represented England the season previous at Wembley as a centre-half. Duncan was from the midlands and had a cheeky brash likable character and wasn't one for enjoying, shall we say, the physical running side of training. This was like most of us to be fair but in Duncan's case he showed his ingenuity during one session in particular that always springs to mind giving me a little chuckle. It was another running session, but this time at the Vauxhall cinder running track. Just off the track on the grass interior, the players had positioned an artificial wall, not a brick wall, but a wall of wooden players who simulated a defensive wall for free-kick practice. On the far side of the running track, our coach stood watching, judging. The session was only for apprentices, so there were about 12 of us in total. During the 12-minute run as we competed and battled against each other and our bodies, Duncan, who had been in the middle of the pack, suddenly out of view of the coach who stood on the far side, ducked behind the wall. As the rest of us completed another grueling lap, Duncan who had been well-rested leapt out from behind the wall where he had been cowering and sprinted to the front of the pack. We didn't know whether to laugh or what. It was an amazing act of cheating which was so obvious to us and surely the coach who would have to be blind not to see it. The problem was that Duncan wasn't a good distance runner and wanted to impress and this was how he thought he could do it. Needless to say he came in for some stick from the lads and although his apprenticeship was for 2 years, he remained until the end of the season only. Duncan was a terrific guy and unfortunately, like many outstanding schoolboy players didn't make it to professional status.

Homesickness as I have mentioned before can be another cause of kids not making it in football. Here we were 16-year-olds, a long way from home in most cases, under the constant pressure of impressing coaches and fitting in with our peers. One of the other apprentices Matthew Bowden from Wales lasted only 3 or 4 weeks before deciding he had seen and done enough and missed home too much. Matthew was another good kid and although not necessarily one of the best players at that point in time, had an opportunity like all of us. If he had got through pre season, the toughest period, who knows? However, we were never to hear from Matt again. There are plenty of stories about the effect of homesickness, for some kids it affects more than others. I think coaches and parents have to be very aware of what's happening in a kid's mind and take the appropriate action.

During my only year as an apprentice, I was still going to school for certain lessons on two days of the week. We lived in Repton close to Luton, which was about a 30-minute walk to my school Cardinal Newman. To help get me there a bit quicker and also to the football club, my Dad bought this old banger of a bike from a neighbour for 5 pounds. I didn't mind and it was great to be able to get to school a bit quicker. Around this time I had read that Manchester City's goalkeeper Joe Corrigan always cycled to and from training. Believing that this was a great way to get fit, I decided to follow suit. Off I'd set through wind and rain all the way to the football club, which was a good 30-minute bike ride. I'd lock my bike up (all 5 pounds worth) underneath one of the stands and go in and get on with my jobs.

Aaron Tighe

Once the lads saw the old bike, I came in for some good humored stick but bravely kept on cycling in learning to defend myself verbally in any clever way I could think of. However, one day as I was about to set off home, I discovered that the unthinkable had happened, my bike had been stolen. Amazed I searched around in case I had made a mistake and left it somewhere else, but my search unturned nothing. A few of the lads Sean Farrell, John Kennedy, Scotty, and co were also making their way out of the ground "Lost something Bizzy?" (I'll explain Bizzy in a minute)" Yeah has anyone seen my bike?" I asked. " You might want to try the bin" came the reply as they rolled around laughing.

True enough there I could see the handlebars of my 5-pound bike sticking out the top of a big yellow skip which was there for construction work. As the lads walked off laughing and I pulled out my bike, I decided that this wasn't a battle I could win and it would have to be the bus from now on. Sometimes you have to cut your losses!

Back to that name Bizzy! The nickname was acquired during my first season as an apprentice. Although still shy around coaches, my sarcastic, take the mickey, side was on full throttle and any chance of 'taking the piss' was fair game. This form of humour was called being 'bizzy' and would normally prefix other words such as 'bollocks' or 'bastard' (please excuse my language, but this was the real world). Hence when you were caught out or on the receiving end of someone's joke, you'd immediately accept defeat calling them a 'bizzy bastard' or 'bizzy bollocks'. Somewhere along the line the second words were dropped and instead of me being called Aaron, Bizzy became my nickname, even amongst the coaches. After a while, this was even shortened to 'Biz'. As nicknames go it was a pretty good one and to this day the name has stuck.

CHRISTMAS WITH A DIFFERENCE

Professional footballers unlike the majority of people don't have a break over Christmas, in fact, the opposite occurs, they get busier. First-team matches are crammed in over the holiday period, taking advantage of the public being on holiday and therefore selling more tickets. For us players, training took place on Christmas day, just like any other in preparation for the first team game that would take place on Boxing Day. Despite the training-as-usual mentality the time of year still got to the players and didn't stop the lads from having a good time.

Steve Foster who was the new club captain and inspirational leader brought some new ideas to the club on the football pitch and also off the football pitch. In the off the pitch category the first introduction was carol singing by the apprentices. A few weeks before Christmas Steve came into the away team dressing room, where we all hung out and got changed and he told us that every single apprentice would have to perform a Christmas Carol in front of the entire playing staff in the home team dressing room at Kenilworth Road. He provided us with a book of songs that we had to select a song from and learn off by heart. Sounds easy so far doesn't it! But here comes the catch. Each singer had to perform the song stark naked standing on a table in the middle of the dressing room with a pair of wellies on and a broom as our microphone! Should anyone not perform, forget their lines or simply be pretty bad, then they would have to suffer the consequences, which was to be shaved and blackened!

To be shaved and blackened was the most feared thing amongst us young lads and was the tactic used by some of the senior players to keep cheeky apprentices under control. We found out one day that they weren't joking around when a couple of the lads were selected for shaving. Hunted down from their hiding place in the boot room one by one, they were dragged out into the middle of the dressing room by some of the seniors, held down, soaped up, and shaved until no curlies were left down below, lying very still at this stage to avoid any accidents with the razor. Of course, this was only the preparation for the blackening, whereby a thick brush of black polish was applied in no gentle manner. I remember a fellow apprentice and great guy who is a black lad also had to endure the shaving on another occasion but instead of black polish, they used white paint stuff which we used to lighten the stripes on football boots. The poor lad like the rest of the lads couldn't get this stuff off for days and hence had to face the giggles of the senior players for some days after in the dressing room. Thank God they never picked on me; I'd have been so embarrassed I'd have died. Looking back this was a pretty shocking practice that guys could hold you down and carry out the shaving and blackening act but amongst the lads, it was all considered good fun, and hopefully, no harm was done. Anyway with the fears embedded in our minds we all made sure we learned our carol lines and melodies apart from the amazing Sean Farrell.

On the morning of the carol-singing contest, we were told that the show was to commence at 9.30am. The worst performer as voted by a show of hands and the receiver of the loudest verbal abuse, would have to do a lap of the Kenilworth Road pitch starkers. A horrible rumour spread amongst the lads that shaving would also be thrown in as part of the fun. The pressure was severely on.

All the apprentices huddled in the small boot room, which adjoined the home team dressing room. A buzz of anticipation built up as we realised that we were actually going to do this and we heard the dressing room fill up with the club's players and coaches, oh yes the coaches as well, they weren't going to miss out on the fun. John Kennedy being probably the maddest out of the bunch was first to go. As the door of the boot room opened and John stepped out in his black wellies and broom in hand, the dressing room shook with the cheer s and laughter. Meanwhile, the rest of us cowered in the safety of the boot room.

Soon it was my turn and facing the laughter and the cheers I rushed out climbed onto the table in the middle of the room and as loudly as I could sang "Deck the Halls with boughs of Holly, Tra la la la la - la la la la, tis the season to be jolly", with that the whole room began to join in on the tra la la bit. I was a success, there was no chance of me being the worst, I was safe, time to enjoy watching the rest of the lads. One by one the lads filed out receiving all sorts of stick and finger-pointing; however, the best was left till last.

Sean Farrell had been an extremely quiet lad before becoming a full-time apprentice. However, his hidden genius was about to be seen and would become legendary in the hearts and minds of anyone who saw him perform. By the time Sean got his hands on the Christmas carol book all of the songs that he recognised had been taken, so he decided to make up his own tune! As the first lines of an attempted wrap version of a carol came out of his mouth, followed by his own "chu, chu" verbal drum effect, we were all in hysterics and I mean hysterics. The pain of laughter was intense, as with all the seriousness in the world he pranced around like George Michael (his favourite), belting out the carol above the roar of the laughter. from that moment on Sean would never be considered the quiet one again, he had arrived.

The good news for us was that no one was shaved that day, however, the worst singer did have to run around the pitch at Kenilworth Road helped by a bucketful of cold water as he started and thankfully I was considered to be the best singer so was safe from the embarrassment (must have been all of those Irish sing songs).

The Christmas carol singing became an institution at Luton. Every year without fail the apprentices had to perform and every year the loser had to run around the pitch. One year Welshman Mark Pembridge, who has gone on to have a terrific career with Clubs like Everton, Fulham, and Benfica, dashed around the pitch starkers, which goes to prove that not all Welshmen are good singers.

After his world-class act in 1985, Sean Farrell went on to star for years to come at Christmas time. Such was his rise, instead of singing a carol, Sean would put on a concert. One year, one of the senior players Danny Wilson created the lighting effects by flicking the dressing room light on and off, a taped recording blasted out "It's been a long time coming, but fresh from his world tour, here' s———————— Fazzy", Hawaii five O music blared out and in came Sean with a cardboard canoe stuck around his middle and his arms paddling a tennis racket through the imagined oceans of the dressing room. As the music finished Faz screamed "Who's Bad (the Michael Jackson catchphrase)" "Fazzies Bad" we all yelled out. This was followed by a rendition of George Michaels ' Faith', with tennis racket replacing the guitar. The stomach pain from laughing was worth it, this was better than Billy Connolly, Freddie Star, and Eddie Murphy all rolled into one. Faz's show was sadly missed when he retired due to having to become a serious role model as a first-team player. Shame but the memories bring a smile to my face.

With Christmas came the traditional Christmas player's parties. A theme was always chosen, bad dress, fancy dress, etc, the date and venue was set and off we'd go. Our first party was probably the most memorable. Cobby, Dave Oldfield, Poutchy and me set off to the local fancy dress shop in Dunstable. I came out with a Gremlin outfit equipped with a fearsome head mask, which received a few wary glances from passers-by as we drove by in Cobby's car. We all met that night in the Sun Do Chinese restaurant in Luton, a popular restaurant for the football team. Many of the lads had already been down the pub during the afternoon, so spirits were already high. The restaurant had laid out a long table to cater for the 40 or so players. Things were going grand until Steve Foster (club captain and leader of the gang) with some senior players decided to get things rolling along at more of a pace, with a yell down the table "All the apprentices have to come down here and down a brandy". That doesn't sound too bad, but when the brandy is a neat full-sized wineglass, things become a bit more interesting. At this stage, I had never ever been drunk or sampled alcohol in any major form (I told you I was shy). "Bizzy, Bizzy, Bizzy, Bizzy" came the chant from the baying crowd of drunken footballers. Reluctantly I made my way to the top of the table where Fozzie handed me the glass filled with Brandy. "Down in one son" Fozzie muttered. To the great joy of the mob, I knocked it back, trying not to think of any consequences. When I sat back down next to my giggling mate Poutchy (who had recently arrived over from Ireland and was doing a part-time schooling thing like I did) my head began to get that light feeling and the world suddenly didn't seem all that real. We were drunk and hey it felt pretty good.

The party continued on at the restaurant for some time and by the time we left making our way towards Ronnelles nightclub, many of these professional athletes would have been better placed in a dry out clinic or a meeting of AA. At Ronnelles, drink got the better of a few people. A young Irish professional attacked senior Irish International Ashley Grimes, landing a Mike Tyson right hand as

Ashley boogied away on the dance floor. Ashley had been giving the player some stick during training and this was the response. Ashley shrugged it off and just kept on dancing. The player continued on his wild spree laughing as he smashed a glass over Mal Donaghy's hard hat. Fortunately for Mal, his fancy dress costume was wisely selected as a World War II German paratrooper with a 'hard hat'. The lad was one of the nicest guys you could meet, the things drink does to you. One of our England Internationals amongst many others could be found in the toilets saying hello to the great white basin but the best happened back at the restaurant. One of the senior players, an England International, never turned up at Ronnelles. The reason being that through his drunken stupor believed that he was a bit of a gymnast. On attempting to do a back flip handstand against the restaurant's front window (he was a big guy), went straight through the glass pane and ended up outside on the street. One of the stalwarts of the 1st team never played for a couple of weeks due to the cuts and abrasions with the public being told that he had Flu. don't always believe what you read in the papers!

There are many stories of Christmas parties and the things that the players got up to but some of them are better kept quiet, like one player sleeping it off in a shopping trolley, three players being unconscious through drink on a coach back from London, fights, loaded drinks, women and much. much more. I think the Christmas party was seen as the release valve for the pressures that players were under and some took it to the max. The next day was always a training day though, the coaches wanted the lads, no matter how bad they felt, to get out on the pitch. Boy did some people suffer.

THE DRINK CULTURE

Certainly during the eighties drink played a large part in the life of 50% + of the football fraternity. At our club alone there was a huge pub culture and it was not unusual to see young and old alike spending entire afternoons and evenings down the local pub socialising and drinking large quantities of alcohol. Many senior players would smuggle bottles of beer into hotel rooms on the night before matches and amazingly as these guys were used to a high level of consumption it appeared that their performance was not diminished to the extent you would expect or at least no obvious visible effects occurred. However high profile premier league players at numerous clubs became alcoholics around this time and even Alex Ferguson at Manchester United discovered when he took over a problematic drink culture.

The life of a footballer is totally unique; you live in a football bubble where everything you do relates to that sport, that way of life, unlike the average person who will go to work the play sport for fun, social activity, or exercise. You generally mix with your teammates because in most cases you don't play in your hometown, so they are the only people you know. As professionals a typical training day may finish at 1 o'clock, so the afternoons and evenings (unless there is a game) are your own and that's a lot of spare time. In my years as a professional, I only knew of two or three players who used that time for education and I was one of those people. Time was killed at the local snooker hall, golf, and videos in front of the telly. Some who needed a little bit more of a stimulant went to the pub or the local bookies. Like I said it's a strange existence. This sounds like an ideal life but some get drawn to far the other way and forget that they live in a privileged profession. I'm sure everyone knows of players who had the talent but wasted it all due to drink or other vices. It sometimes makes me laugh when I meet ex-players who will say "Yeah I was pretty good, could have made it but got into the drinking and all that" like it's something to brag about. What a load of rubbish.

On a lighter note, as I mentioned snooker halls, I'll tell you about a memorable moment during a game between me and David Oldfield. David was an athletic tall center-forward who had broken into the first team and after only 9 or so games was attracting serious interest from other top-flight clubs including Man City. They had offered Luton 700,000 pounds for Dave and the club was happy to cash in. It was simply up to Dave to decide which club to go to. As we played snooker David was left with a difficult shot on the pink. Stepping back and thinking for a moment, he then calmly stated "If I pot this ball I'm going to Man City, If I miss I'm staying at Luton". With that, he leaned down over the table, pulled the cue back as far as he could and launched the cue like a bazooka at the white. The white took off at a lightning pace and smashed into the pink, which missed the proposed pocket by miles but carried on its journey, rebounding off two cushions before making the long trip back down the table towards the open-mouthed David and the corner pocket. "Will it or won't it reach" we silently questioned ourselves, both of us thinking exactly the same thing. Losing pace the pink crept towards the pocket, finally dropping over the edge into the awaiting net. If ever fate was telling somebody to do something, this was it. David signed for Man City within a week and all because of a snooker shot!

THE GYM

The Oak Road stand at Luton's Kenilworth Road ground is positioned behind a goal, to the left-hand side as you walk out of the player's tunnel. Directly behind the stand butting up against the old structure are the Oak Road 1930's red-bricked terraced houses. Splitting the houses below are rickety blue metal staircases that twist down from the top of the stand to the laneways that lie between the houses. The clunk of trainers against the metal staircase echoed in the small confined space, as we'd descend to my favourite football hideaway 'the Gym'.

The Gym was a 20-metre by 15-metre room tucked away underneath the Oak Road stand. The room in its original form had a red-painted concrete floor, with brown wooden gymnasium wall bars fixed to the, as you entered, right-hand alcove wall. The battered asbestos ceiling sloped dramatically from left to right following the contours of the stand. Big chunks of roofing and dust would rain down when a ball was inadvertently struck against the ceiling. On the top left apex wall, metal meshing covered broken windows. The dim light crept in like some Speilburg sci-fi movie. A rope representing a tennis net hung between the centre left and right walls. The rope could be raised to volleyball level for games of head tennis, or left at tennis level for a game of volleys (feet-only game). On the back wall, the outline of a goal was painted in white, with numbers from 1 to 5 painted in boxes representing targets for shooting practice. It was a kid footballer's dream. It was my blue gate and Green in Banbury, my road sign and back garden wall in Dublin all rolled into one.

After and before training, hours were spent competing and battling in competitions with the other guys in this room. David Oldfield and myself in particular had roaring competitive volleys matches, using table tennis scoring to keep track of the impending winner. A spinned shot with the outside of your foot could kill off the point if placed accurately underneath a wall bar, and defensive positions were established similar to a squash player. Reactions had to be lightning-fast. The level of skill achieved in this environment was phenomenal and before long a full range of spinning and control techniques were developed. The hours upon hours spent competing heightened my ball control to a new level. The gym was my domain and I was unstoppable. I loved the individual competition, the emphasis purely on myself to win. When everyone else was going or gone home, me and the dedicated David Oldfield would exhaustedly make our way back to the changing rooms.

After a few years, the room was deemed unsafe due to the battered asbestos roof, and a face-lift was undertaken. The artificial pitch replaced the red concrete floor, a safe ceiling was installed and the old brown wall bars were discarded. The walls were painted a bright white and new lights were installed brightening the room. I sometimes think about the amount of dust that we breathed in during those old days. let's hope it wasn't too much!

MY COUNTRY CALLS

In my experience, there is no prouder feeling than to represent your country in sport. I had represented Ireland at schoolboy level and whilst in my first full year at a professional club, was now asked to represent Ireland at youth level. However, there was a problem. I was suffering from an ankle injury. I had been out of action for a week or so with damaged ligaments. David Pleat the manager at the time was not willing to let me go and play unless I could prove my fitness.

It was agreed that if I came through a local youth five-a-side competition okay, then I could travel the following day to Ireland for the game. I convinced John Faulkener our youth team coach that I would be okay to play, even though I hadn't trained for ages. In the dressing room before our first game, I strapped the ankle myself as tight as I could, to prevent any movement sideways. I figured that if I couldn't roll it I could live with any pain that it gave me. The ankle felt as weak as hell but playing for Ireland was too important an opportunity to miss. The indoor five-a-side game started and eager to prove my fitness I got a couple of early tackles in. The game went well and the strapping held firm. Although painful, I had managed to hide the injury. John gave me the nod to travel and off I went to represent Ireland.

Despite the plane landing virtually sideways on the Cork runway, I arrived in Ireland safe and sound. We trained the next morning and once again I strapped my ankle as firm as I could. After the session, Noel O'Reilly the manager called me to one side. "Aaron, how would you like to be Captain tomorrow?" Well, the answer was obvious and in an instant, I felt like I had just grown another 6 inches. Noel who had never seen me play before had been impressed in training and it was now my good fortune to lead the team, I was so proud.

The game was a friendly youth international against Northern Ireland and was one of only two Youth international fixtures for my age group. Northern Ireland was considered the favourites for the fixture as they apparently had an experienced side out. We had a few familiar faces from our schoolboy days, goalkeeper Andy Farrell, Curtis Fleming, Derek Mcardle, and Pat Fenlon. However Derek, me and Andy were the only ones remaining from the schoolboy International team, which I thought was such a shame. I mean what happened to all the other talented lads?

In the dressing room before the game at the Mardyke in Cork, an official came in explaining that the Captain was required to wear an armband. The coaches searched frantically but there wasn't one in the kit bag. Instead, they wrapped a piece of bandage around my arm and pinned it with a safety clip. As I lead the team out onto the pitch, I was truly the proudest bloke on the planet. The ground although only small was packed and there was a buzz of expectation. We stood for the national anthems with chests out and shoulders back, soaking up the realisation that we were representing our country, one of the best moments for me. We then broke for a team photo. While the lads continued their warm-up, I went up for the toss and exchanged pennants with the Northern Ireland Captain. We won the kick off and I stood directly behind our two centre-forwards Pat Fenlon and Kevin Nugent. As they kicked off passing the ball back to me I paused with the ball for a brief moment. The two Northern Ireland forwards enthusiastically came charging towards me. Quickly I surged into the gap between them and using my old Ricky Mc Evoy trick moving the ball from one foot to the other and back again, maneuvered my way sweetly between them before passing the ball to one of my teammates. It was an attacking start, which signaled the way we were going to play the game. The pain that I was getting from my tightly strapped ankle didn't bother me 'I was Captain of my country'!

We went on to win the game convincingly 3 - 1 and I assisted in two of the goals, the first a flick-on header after a forward run and the second a free kick played left-footed into the penalty area. Goalkeeper Andy Farrell an old teammate of mine at Stella Maris pulled off some terrific saves that helped keep the opposition out, making it a game to remember and a great win for us, particularly as we were considered the underdogs. My centre-midfield partner on the day was a lad from Dundalk football club called 'Steve Staunton'. His name would appear on the Liverpool first team sheet in years to come. He was a quiet lad and would amaze us all with his sudden surge to the big time. Steve was a late arrival in England a similar story to that of Roy Keane. After the game, as I entered the dressing room, the camaraderie and spirit shown by the lads touched a nerve and my emotions got the better of me as I found myself fighting back tears of pride for a job well done. How I loved playing for my country.

THE JOHN MOORE ERA

Towards the end of our first full season at Luton David Pleat and first-team coach Trevor Hartley left the club for Tottenham Hotspur. Whenever there is a change of manager at a club, there is an air of anticipation. Who's going to take over? Will he like me as a player? will my chances improve or decrease?, now I have to prove myself all over again etc! David Pleat was a big fan of Aaron Tighe as a kid. He liked the way I played. When during the season I wasn't selected for some youth cup matches (I was still playing a year underage), he contacted my parents and assured them that I was still on track. He also asked us to play the game in a way, that suited my style down to the ground, passing and moving, one-touch two-touch. So it came as a shock to us to learn of his departure and waited anxiously for the arrival of the new manager. Although various well-known names were banded about, the job was given to Reserve team manager John Moore.

John was an outstanding football coach. His Scottish rough accent resonated with passion and determination whenever he spoke. No longer were we to address John as 'John'. His new name was Boss and that took a little getting used to. John was backed up by two new coaches in the season of 1986/87, Jim Ryan, an x Luton Town and Manchester United player and Ray Harford, a well-respected coach who had I believe enjoyed a successful management spell at Fulham. Ray became the first team coach and Jim took on the mantle of reserve team coach.

The team that John inherited as manager was exceptional and achieved in his first and only season in charge a highly respected 6th place in the top flight. However, all was not well. Firstly, although getting results Luton was not the attractive passing side that the fans were used to. This could possibly be put down to the influence of Ray Harford. Somewhere along the line John and the players lost the attractive passing style of play and Ray's influence on the team tactics took over. Before long the team was being asked to play a more direct style. Full-backs were encouraged to play long balls over opposition full-backs down the line or alternatively long high-angled balls to the furthest centre-forward. Playing from the back wasn't encouraged so much as could be 'too dangerous'. In one training session in which I was involved David Preece a skillful midfielder asked, "So you want us to play like Ireland?" "Yes" replied Ray. David shook his head as he walked away. Hey now don't get me wrong, there's nothing wrong with playing direct but it wasn't Luton's style, and the players and the fans didn't like it. They had been brought up on the flowing short passing one-touch two-touch style of David Pleat. Ray would tell us that "I want to play like Liverpool and they play long balls first to stretch the game and then short balls". This may have been true but Luton's style just went one-dimensional. There simply wasn't the same movement but the results came and the 1st team fished its highest position ever so you can't knock it.

After just one season in charge, John Moore resigned, despite achieving Luton's most successful ever season. Player power and the pressures of the job, it would appear, were too much. Rumours suggested that John just didn't enjoy all the political crap that goes on at that high level. Ray Harford assumed the manager's role and it appeared that no love was lost between the two.

Before he left, John had a meeting with me as my contract was coming to an end. The big question was whether or not I would be retained as a player. I was 17 years old soon to turn 18 and was now firmly established in the reserve team. Our season had once again been hugely successful in the youth team, winning the Southern Junior Floodlit Cup, which was considered the FA Youth Cup for the south of England.

During these cup competitions, I had managed to excel. These games were showpiece events for youth players, playing under lights at the top grounds and stadiums with managers and scouts from all the top clubs watching. Although apprehensive going into these games, we understood that these were the games you had to impress in and fortunately, I rose to the occasion. One of my finest ever performances as a footballer was during a semifinal with Tottenham Hotspur at Luton's Kenilworth Road. I always loved playing under the floodlights, it always gave the illusion that you were running faster and the ball seemed to zip along a bit quicker. In this particular game, I was playing centre-midfield, my favourite position. Tottenham's Vinnie Samways was my opponent, an enormously skillful lad who had been playing in the Tottenham first team from a very young age. I can recall reading that Vinnie was earning some amazing amount of money and to psyche myself up I got my mind into a jealous state saying "he's not better than me" and I was going to prove it. John Faulkener our youth team coach was a terrific guy and encouraged me to get the ball whenever I could. During the match I just seemed to attract the ball, putting hardly a pass wrong and tackling Vinni like a demon. We won the game by an emphatic 3 - 0 margin. After the game David Coates our former coach commented to me and my parents "What a display of passing and tackling, kid you've got a very big future". I went home on cloud nine, I was the man of the moment, life was good, my hard work was paying off and I was going to be a 'player'.

A couple of weeks later during a reserve team match at Portsmouth, disaster on a scale that wouldn't be realised until years later struck. Jim Ryan was playing me at left back in the reserves, which was a very comfortable position for me as it allowed me time to use my passing, dribbling, and crossing ability. The success of my performances in this position was also recognised in the press by Manager Ray Harford as he stated that I would make a future classy left back, very nice thank you.

We received a free kick deep in our half and as I struck through the ball with my left foot, I received a sudden jolt of excruciating pain in my left thigh muscle. The pain was from deep inside the leg and could be compared to being hit by a big rock smack bang in the thigh. Hobbling over to Jim Ryan, I apologetically said "Jim I've got to come off, I think I've pulled a muscle". I can recall the journey back to Luton being extremely uncomfortable on the coach. Our physio had compressed my leg in a mummified type of bandage and the pain was bad. The next day in the treatment room we unraveled the bandage to check the damage. W here my thigh muscle had once been, there was now a gaping valley. The muscle had ruptured completely; this wasn't going to heal in a couple of days let alone a couple of weeks. The bad news was that the final of the youth cup was taking place in a few days at Stamford Bridge. We were pitted against Chelsea but there was no way I was going to be fit. It was a major disappointment as I was playing extremely well and I really wanted to put on a show against the club I turned down to join Luton from high up in Stamford Brigade's main stand I watched the final take place. The lads beat the Chelsea youth team 2 - 1 which was a good result for the first leg. Despite frantic efforts to try and build up the leg for the second leg on the plastic at Kenilworth Road, we failed by a long way and once again I watched this time from the bench. The lads won emphatically 4 - 0 and we were now the best youth team in the south of England and arguably England. It was a fantastic achievement for Luton but showed the quality of players that we had and the outstanding coaching and guidance that we had received.

So here I was sitting in front Of the Boss John Moore to talk about whether or not I had a future at the club. "ehhh, so kid how do you think you've done this season?" came the question "Some Good, Boss and some not so good" I replied "well son, I'm offering you a one-year professional contract and we'll pay you 120 pound a week. It's purely down to your performance in the semifinal against Tottenham, is that Okay?" Is that okay really meant, that's all your getting and you will agree or else. The 120 pound a week was a shocker as it meant that we were actually coming out with slightly less money than when we were apprentices, as no expenses were paid for accommodation when you were a pro. Timidly I replied, "Yes Boss, thank you Boss". All the way home I was kicking myself because everyone had been saying that we should get a signing fee upfront but I had been too scared to ask.

When I got home I decided that this was stupid and that I should ask the question. I rang the club and eventually was put through to the Boss. "Hello" came the gruff voice down the phone. Rather than a pleasant hello, it was more like a threatening hello, which meant, say the wrong thing and you'll die a horrible death. "Hi Boss, I was wondering if I get a signing on fee?" "NO, see you at training" came the brisk reply. With that, the line was disconnected and all my time spent thinking about how should I ask had been overwhelmed by a two-second dismissal. Hey, at least I asked!

THE STIFFS

"Would you rather be, in a factory" sang Jimmy Ryan the reserve team manager. This was his regular line during training. Jim was truly still a kid at heart and loved being part of football. Another Scotsman, Jim had an amazing background in football. At his first training session with us, he concentrated on ball skills and showed immediately that he knew what he was talking about, demonstrating techniques and skills with ease. Jim joined Manchester United as an apprentice alongside the legendary George Best. The two of them developed together at United culminating with Jim sitting on the bench at the European Cup win in 1966 whilst Best starred. I found his stories of Manchester United days enthralling. They were first-hand stories about people who I had only read about, the club with which I had been a fanatical supporter, and finally stories about the great Matt Busby, the legendary manager of Man Utd. Jim would tell us about how shy Best was as a 16-year-old, as they began to go to clubs with Jim having to do all the talking to the girls. He told us of how dedicated he and Best were, continually staying behind to practice shooting and crossing and scoring directly from corners. He told us of how Busby was seen as a larger-than-life figure at Man Utd and how scared they were to approach the man.

After one particular Luton v Man Utd game, I was standing in the player's lounge with Jim, when a sudden hush became noticeable in the crowded room. George Best had entered and just for that split second, everyone stopped talking. I was delighted when he came over and started talking to Jim. It was great to be in the presence of such a legend.

Jim's management style was 'he was one of the lads'. On his first day at the club, he came into the away team dressing room. The away team dressing room was where the reserves got changed, as opposed to the first team who occupied the home team dressing room. Jim came in carrying a bag of doughnuts. "There you go lads, get stuck in" he said in his light Scottish accent. It was his way of getting established amongst the lads and it worked, I mean this guy wasn't scary at all.

Jim wanted us to play football the right way and he inherited a reserve team, which was filled with the successful youth teams of the previous few years. We would tear reams apart at times playing some exciting pass and move attacking football. I can recall a run of games where we took on a strong Arsenal side at home followed by Southampton and Portsmouth away. The Arsenal team was filled with a number of big-name stars but they came totally unstuck going down 6 - 1 to our overwhelming performance. I managed to top one of the six and as I walked off the pitch I smiled at Jim saying "Nice one for you Jim". We then went down to Southampton, another team with a strong youth policy. Southampton had developed players at the time like Le Tissier, Shearer and the Wallace brothers. We ran out 7 - 0 winners with me scoring a diving header and a long drive that hit the net low and hard. This was followed by another 7 - 0 at Portsmouth. These were terrific results in a competitive environment and showed what a strong squad we had.

After the Arsenal result, the local newspaper 'the Luton News' published a letter from a dissatisfied supporter. In the letter, he described how he had given up on watching the poor quality football that the first team was playing and taken to watching the exciting passing attacking football that was on display from the reserves. Sean Farrell (Faz) pinned it up on the first team dressing room noticeboard for all to see. When Jim found out he stormed in ripping it down from the wall. Why, you may ask? The reason is simple, a first-team manager under pressure may find it threatening that the reserve team manager is getting such praise, not good politics if you know what I mean.

Jim totally wanted us to play good football. Even if we lost he was happy as long as we performed well. Alternatively, sometimes we won but we'd get a right old bollocking in the dressing room cause the performance was poor. The result didn't matter, the way we played did.

On one occasion Brian Talbot, the youth team coach of Watford, brought his entire youth team to Kenilworth Road to watch us in action. He wanted to show his kids how to play the right way. What a compliment for us lads.

Playing in the reserves had a life cycle, which began as an exciting adventure. You were launched as a 16-year-old into men's football for the first time, playing with and against some excellent players, who were either coming to the end of their careers, or coming back from injury or fighting their way back into the first team. Of course, these players were mixed with the youngsters who were also trying to impress and be recognised for first-team action. However, if you found yourself in the reserves as an older professional, it was not a good feeling. It was like not being allowed to play with the popular kids because you weren't good enough. As an older Pro it was not the place to stay for long.

I recall playing a home game against Southampton in one of my first reserve games. In the dressing room before the game, I'd always have a look at the away team's team sheet to check out who was playing. On this occasion, we were up against the fearsome centre-forward 'Joe Jordan'. Joe Jordan had been one of my heroes at Manchester United and here I was sharing the same field. These were the moments to cherish. Fellow Irishman Marcus Tuite a nippy right midfielder made us all laugh early in the game. Joe Jordan had received the ball on the halfway line. As he moved forward with the ball, Marcus over-enthusiastically came from nowhere and swiped big Joe Jordan's legs from under him. As Jordan rose looking more like a snarling wolf than a footballer, little Marcus sprinted in the opposite direction, making sure that he stayed out of Jordan's way for the rest of the game. As the final whistle blew I made sure that I was the first player to shake the great man's hand. Another childhood dream come true.

The following pre-season, I was flying. I had worked extremely hard in the close season to maintain a high level of fitness. This was going to be my season and the sooner the better. During a practice session involving the first team and Manager Ray Harford at Vauxhalls training ground, enthusiasm and determination were running high. Whilst going for a 50/50 ball with Faz, I just nudged the ball beyond him but his momentum carried forward and with an almighty clash his knee smashed into my left thigh. As I spun in the air, the jolt of pain struck hard. Hitting the ground, I thought my leg was broken, the pain was excruciating, I rolled from side to side and a compressed scream yelped from my mouth. Ray Harford was first to get to me, with Faz and a few other players looking on concerned. All they could do was just let me lie there until I stopped rolling and managed to control the pain. What seemed like an eternity passed and soon I was being carried to the team coach to be taken back to the medical room at Kenilworth Road.

The good news was the leg wasn't broken. However, the bad news was that there was severe damage to the thigh muscle. To make things worse, this was the same muscle that we had just nurtured back from the rupture a few months before. All my hard work had just gone down the drain. It was back to the drawing board for Aaron Tighe. Recover I did but things were never to be the same. Despite the best warm-ups before playing and training, the muscles began to tear on different occasions, interrupting the flow of consistency that is required to make the first team. Interspersed with this were some excellent performances with a terrific bunch of players. I can recall Gary Cobb who played on the right side of midfield and me mainly on the left having a competition to see who would score the most goals in the season. Cobby ran out a narrow winner scoring 16 goals to my 15. Cobby got a few runs in the first team due to his reserve team performances but my inconsistency and the strong left-sided first-team players Kingsley Black and David Preece kept me out of contention.

This was the season of 1988. Luton Town was flying. They reached the final of the Simod Cup, a national cup competition that was introduced around this period; they also reached the final of the League Cup and the semifinal of the FA Cup. With two Wembley finals already booked, Luton narrowly went down to Wimbledon in the FA Cup semi-final at White Hart Lane 2 - 1, a bitterly disappointing result as Luton had taken a 1 - 0 lead through Mick Harford. Wimbledon famously went on to beat Liverpool in the final. The Simod Cup final at Wembley was next and although strong favourites against a lower-division Reading team, Luton came mightily unstuck losing 4 - 1 on the day. It was a lesson in the error of pushing a flat back four too high up the pitch, when not in possession. Reading had a clever winger by the name of John Smylie who continually made darting runs in behind Luton full-back Tim Breacker. The Reading midfielders without even looking kept delivering the ball into acres of space behind the Luton defender. The good news was, Luton learned the lesson for the big final against Arsenal in the League Cup.

The FA Cup final is without doubt the major final in England due to its history and the fact that every club in England from amateurs right through to the top clubs have a chance to win it. It's a romantic trophy to win. However, during the eighties, the League Cup was still a major trophy. Unlike the nineties where clubs began to field lessened teams due to fixture commitments.

Luton were up against George Graham's much-fancied Arsenal. As I watched from the Wembley stand, I turned to Mick Obrien, a Dublin lad with outstanding talent "Mick, we'll be out there soon, me and you". I felt it with such belief, from deep inside I believed that my destiny lay in being a successful professional footballer at the highest level. There was no reason for me not to make it. I knew I had the talent, I just had to consistently prove it .

Kingsley Black, one of our fellow youth team players from my first year at the club, played in the final. Kingsley had established himself in the team as an exciting left-winger with deft ball control and an ability to beat players with a terrific balance that sometimes left defenders literally on their backside. Kingsley was the shyest footballer I ever met and a lovely guy. Before the game in the Wembley dressing room, he was so nervous that he couldn't sign autographs due to his hand shaking so much. Kingsley had proven to us all that the first team was there for the taking. How I wished I was out on that pitch.

After an amazing finish to the game, Luton conquered the mighty Arsenal. The club had won its first major title and under the leadership of Ray Harford. It was a huge success which left us all excited and in a party atmosphere at the Savoy Hotel in London that evening. Dressed in a black tie and ready to congratulate all the lads, a lingering disappointment hung in the background. My thoughts kept returning to the fact that I could have been out there. Call it jealousy or whatever; I was determined to be there the next time. A lot of work would have to be done.

DAVID PLEAT TO THE RESCUE

Up to the point of the serious thigh injuries my career appeared to be on track with some exciting reserve team performances. However a season of inconsistency due to regularly being sidelined had taken its toll and At the age of 19, it appeared that my career was floundering. Although a regular in the reserves when fit, there was no sign of first-team football. Ray Harford was still the manager and simply hadn't seen anything in me that was going to improve his first team. One day late in the season I was called over to talk to him after a training session. "Son, David Pleat has asked if you'd like to go up to Leicester on a month's loan, I think it's a good idea. He wants you up there tonight for a reserve match. What do you think?" My heart skipped a beat with excitement. David Pleat had always appreciated my ability and for the first time in ages, I felt like I was being recognised. It felt like a fantastic opportunity. "I'd love to go I replied".

I borrowed my Dad's red Astra and set off on the hour-long trek up the M1 motorway. Once at Leicester's Filbert Street ground, I reported directly to David Pleat. He explained that he was giving me an opportunity to impress and that it was likely I would only be involved in the reserve team. After the meeting, I had a couple of hours spare, so I had a sleep on the medical bench in the dressing room. Come match time I was introduced to the lads and I was buzzing. I was totally focused and determined to do well. I understood the importance of this month's trial. It had to work.

The game kicked off and the centre-forward passed the ball instantly out to the right-winger, who set off on a terrific attacking run. The move developed until finally, I found myself sprinting to the edge of the box, the ball was crossed and with my first touch, I volleyed the ball right-footed high into the roof of the net. Wow, what a start! my first touch for Leicester in the first few seconds of the game was a goal. Nothing was going to stop me after that. In my favourite centre-midfield position, I took control of the game in a way that I hadn't come near for a long time at Luton. The game was an outstanding success. My confidence was sky-high. I was a wanted man!

The following game was away at Elland Road the home of Leeds United. We gained a free kick outside their box early on. Nobody seemed to want it, so I quickly picked up the ball and placed it down. Taking a short run I managed to bend the ball up and over the wall into the top corner inches away from the diving goalkeeper. Aaron Tighe was playing like a superstar! After this game, reports got back to Ray Harford that I was performing exceptionally well. The next game away at Coventry was attended by John Faulkener our youth team coach at Luton. I had an absolute stormer and was playing the best football of my life. This then lead to the next game, a home match against a strong Nottingham Forest side. On hearing about my success to date. The game was attended by Luton manager Ray Harford and chief scout Ron Howard. It was as if they had to see my performances to believe them. Although I didn't know it I had saved my best for this last game, from my centre-midfield position, I was constantly on the ball and my passing both short and long was second to none. Although I didn't score I did crash a shot against the bar from some 35 yards out. My confidence was even higher by this stage and I felt like I could do no wrong. I took on the playmaker role while Paul Groves the other midfielder made the attacking runs. My performances were proof of how much confidence can do for a player.

My time at Leicester was a complete refresh for me and my performances showed this. I roomed with a few of the other young lads including Paul Kitson who went on to have a good career with Newcastle and West Ham and we all got on pretty well. Jimmy Quinn, a Northern Ireland International, who wasn't fitting into the first-team plan at the time, would always pick me first for the 5-a-side competition which was a great testament to how I was performing. The star player at Leicester at the time was Scotland International Gary Mc Allister. Gary was a special player. On one occasion during training, Mike Newell a former Luton centre-forward blatantly fouled me. Turning to the coach for some help, I received a "get on with it" reply. Fuming I went after the ball like a madman. The unfortunate Gary Mac who had just received the ball, took the full force of my wild booted swing "Take it easy son, take it easy son" he shouted, looking at me with surprised 'this kid mad' eyes. My confidence was so high I was happy to fight anyone, I saw myself as a match for anybody at this stage.

After suffering a badly bruised toe in the Nottingham Forest game, an injury attained whilst nutmegging Forrest's Phil Starbuck, I found myself laid up on the medical room table receiving treatment. David Pleat came into the room and approached me. "I'm thinking about making Luton an offer for you, maybe 70,000 or something like that, what do you think?" The question amazed me. "Yeah, it sounds good Boss" I replied. Pleat had a way of looking you right in the eye to gauge your reaction to his questions. It was obvious that he was testing me out to see if I was keen to sign with Leicester. "I'll think about it, I'll think about it," he said as he walked away. Pleat apparently had tried to extend my loan period but Luton on seeing my performances wanted me back straight away.

Disappointed that I was going back to Luton after only a month, I had a brief conversation with Leicester's first team coach Gordon Lee. Gordon had been Everton Manager during the seventies and was more importantly manager during the years that I had supported them as a little fella, so it was amazing to just be having a conversation with the guy. "You never know son, the first team might get an injury or two and you could be playing in the Cup Final next month, so don't think of it as a bad thing going back. It could work out for you". It was true; Luton had reached the League Cup final for the second year on the trot and was up against a strong Nottingham Forest team. At the time though I just couldn't see it happening and I was proved right.

On my return to Luton, I was treated like a hero. Ray Harford greeted me like the prodigal son. Putting his arm around me he said, "Well done son, I'd never noticed you before, but it's like I've found a new player, welcome back". Although confident in my ability, I never recaptured that scintillating form I had at Leicester. However, the first team would call but not in time for the Wembley final.

The reward for my efforts at Leicester was a negotiated further three-year contract at Luton. To think that before I went to Leicester I was likely to be released by Luton at the end of the season, this was some turnaround. When the offer was made to me, I wasn't totally comfortable. I had seen no first team action with the club and had felt like a different person whilst at Leicester. I can recall taking a long walk up Luton's beautiful Warden Hill countryside, balancing out the pro's and cons of staying at Luton or moving to Leicester permanently. David Pleat made the decision an easy one. Once the offer was on the table from Luton, I rang Pleat asking for his advice. "Boss, they've offered me a three-year contract with 15,000 signing-on fee spread over the three years along with 250 pounds a week climbing to 350 a week and a 5000 loyalty fee at the end, what do you think I should do?" The question was almost a plea for him to say "Well we'll match it, son, come to us" But instead came the reply "They've offered you a good deal son, take it" As I put down the phone, I was a little disappointed but at the same time realised that my mind had been made up for me, I was to remain at Luton, who was after all a division higher than Leicester. Time would tell if it was a good move.

I TACKLED LIAM BRADY

With my recent success at the club level, it was great to also receive the news that I was required to play for the Republic of Ireland Under 21's in the annual Toulon tournament in France. The competition was to be held during the summer break and the squad was asked to report for a few days of training in Dublin before flying to France. This was 1989 and the Irish people had grown fanatical about the Irish team. Jack Charlton the England World Cup hero was manager and had claimed saint status by not only taking the team to the European Championship finals but by doing the unthinkable, leading Ireland to a victory over England during that same tournament. In 1989 Ireland was flying in their World Cup qualifying matches. At the time we met, the senior team was also in training for an important qualifier against Malta. To my delight, we trained together.

The Irish team at the time was made up of some of my footballing heroes, people like Liam Brady, Frank Stapleton, Kevin Moran, David O'Leary and Paul McGrath. The likes of Ray Houghton, Ronnie Whelan, and John Aldridge were at the time members of the great Liverpool team of the eighties. It was great to be in their company.

During a practice match, I had the pleasure of playing against the great Liam Brady in midfield. Brady was coming to the end of his career at this stage but still looked a class apart from the rest. Here I was playing against a man who had made me cry with his skill in the 1979 FA Cup final between Man U and Arsenal. United had dramatically clawed back a 2 - 0 deficit in the last 5 minutes of the game. My Uncle Des and me were watching in ecstasy in my Nana' s house in Crumlin Dublin. However, we soon began to cry as Brady weaved some magic before creating an Arsenal winner in the dying seconds. Brady then of course went on to win a championship with the mighty Italian giants Juventus. In short, he was a legend.

During the practice match, I amazed myself by tackling the legend himself and winning the ball away from him. I can still see Liam's face with the expression of "Who the hell are you kid?" All I knew was that it was now safe to retire. I had lived out my childhood dreams!

The evening before we were due to travel to France, I went with my brother Derek to watch the senior team play Malta at Lansdowne Road Dublin. It was a full house with a party atmosphere. The fans were doing the Mexican wave, Irish football was buzzing, and it felt like nothing could go wrong. As the lads stood for the national anthem, I watched, convinced that it was my fate to be out there with them. I had proven that I had the talent and all I required was the consistency to make it happen. I always remember our youth coach John Faulkener saying, "Being a good player isn't important, being a consistently good player is". The amazing thing was that if I impressed the following season, there was every possibility that I could be considered for the World Cup in 1990. I knew that I was far away from it, but a regular first-team player in the top flight of England would have to be looked at.

We arrived in Toulon the following day. Amongst the players included were some of my old teammates, Ricky Mc Evoy who was playing League of Ireland football after being released by Luton and fellow Luton reserve player Neil Poutch. We were also joined by some under 15/18 compadriates like Curtis Fleming (league of Ireland), Eddie Gormley (league of Ireland), Derek Brazil (Man Utd), and Steve Staunton (Liverpool). Steve was one of a few lads who were part of the senior squad but travelled with the under 21's as well.

Mark Kelly (Portsmouth) who was a terrific young winger at the time and who had a handful of senior international appearances became my roommate for the tournament. Mark was a great lad and we got on famously. Unfortunately, he pulled a muscle during our first training session and took no part in the tournament.

The manager of the under 21' s was 'Maurice Setters'. Maurice was an English guy and was Jack Charlton's right-hand man with the senior team. I happened to be in the hotel reception when Maurice arrived. I was shocked to see the attitude of other officials on his arrival. A particular coach could be seen running over to him to pick up and carry his suitcases. It was like God had arrived and his servants were waiting. It was embarrassing stuff and I certainly lost respect for these people. You really had to see it to believe it. I never would have imagined grown men could act in such a manner. I mean there's brown nosing and there's brown-nosing!

When the team was announced for the first game, I was extremely disappointed not to be included in the starting lineup. True, Maurice hadn't seen me perform before but I still believed I should have been in the team. The team had a poor start drawing with Senegal 0 - 0. The next day during a practice game, I found my best form and stole the show. The lads voted me the man of the match and sure enough, this earned me a place in the centre of Midfield, my favourite position against Bulgaria.

As I stood in the lineup singing along to the Irish national anthem, I was determined to do a great job. However, we found ourselves chasing the Bulgarians, who were a decent side and who would go on to reach the final. Despite us having the experienced Niall Quinn and David Kelly up front, we just couldn't get our passing together. The Bulgarians were playing an attractive passing game and we were just lumping it. Disappointed with my inability to get much of the ball, I received more disappointment by being substituted with ten minutes to go. The score was 1 - 0 to Bulgaria at the time and pretty soon after became 2 - 0 as the Bulgarians showed no mercy. My mate Neil Poutch said to me after the game "At least you were trying to get the ball down to play". It summed it up. My international ventures to this point had been exciting affairs but this was pure frustration.

ME A DUTCH INTERNATIONAL

The next day myself, Ricky Mc Evoy and another lad from Tottenham were asked to take part in an international 11 against France. The Dutch team was forced to pull out of the tournament due to an appalling plane crash in Amsterdam where hundreds had been killed. It was agreed that the international 11 would take their place. The three of us were joined by three England players, Marco Gabbiadini, Gary Charles, and Guy Butters, 3 Bulgarians, plus players from Senegal and another African country, which I can't quite remember.

The Senegal manager, a Frenchman, did his best before the game to organise us into some sort of team. The French were a favourite to win the tournament and showed plenty of class in the first half with players like David Ginola and Desailly. However, for all their possession and chances could not turn the ball into the net. The amazing thing was, that one of the African outfield players was playing in Goal for us and didn't have a clue. The ball was hitting off his knee and bouncing out, he was dropping crosses but there was always someone to clear. How the ball never went in was truly amazing. Meanwhile, I was loving the game. The pressure was off as it was just a makeshift outfit and these players didn't know how to lump it. I was playing in the middle of the park and receiving passes from deep within our half. I had time to get the ball and play long 40/50 yard passes out wide to Gabbiadini, who'd taken a position out wide on the right. It was great fun and although competitive, I did receive a kick up the backside from a frustrated Frenchman, it was thoroughly enjoyable. It felt like I was back at Leicester.

The first half ended 0-0 and in the dressing room at Half time our international 11 manager explained how he felt we might even win the game if we pushed up a bit. A few changes were made to the side to give everyone a game and out we went for the second half. Whereas everything they hit stayed out in the first half, this half everything went in. It was like the Alamo as the French ripped us apart scoring 6 goals to our one reply. As per the first half, I enjoyed the second, achieving a classic nutmeg just outside my box, "nuts" came the shout from Gary Charles who was positioned just outside me. I also hit a cracking 35-yard shot, which got a rousing round of applause from the local partisan crowd. It was fun football again but it brought disappointing news. The fact that we played in the game meant we weren't going to be selected for the next Ireland game against England. But looking back, if I hadn't played, I could never say that I played for Holland!

FRUSTRATIONS BOIL OVER

s a youngster, I was a shy lad, as I've mentioned numerous times. I'd follow the rule and toe the line. As I moved into my late teens, I began to question people's decisions, particularly if I felt they were at the detriment of my career. On two occasions prior to my Leicester trip, I found myself storming off the pitch in reserve games after being substituted by Jim Ryan. The fact was that I deserved to be subbed, but at the time I had developed this anger inside which was fuelled by a feeling that I wasn't being given a fair go. I was seeing certain players who I felt I was every bit as good as, getting opportunities in the first team and here I was being subbed in the reserves. After one such occasion, I met with Jim Ryan and John Faulkener the two junior coaches. Eddie Corcoran the scout from Dublin was over and he could see that I was getting frustrated, hence the arranged meeting. "I was just giving Ceri Hughes a run Aaron, that's all," said Jim innocently. At the time I thought there was a vendetta against me but the reality was that younger players had to be developed as well. My frustration was born out of my inconsistent performances. The reason for this inconsistency can be put down to injuries and confidence. At Leicester I was wanted so I played out of my skin. At Luton, I was just one of the young prospects and my form was hit and miss.

This anger and frustration boiled over on a memorable, for the wrong reasons, occasion in Toulon. After sitting on the bench for the England game, which was drawn 0 - 0, I was selected to play against a French B team. Setters the coach put me down for a wide left role, a position that I never liked playing as I wasn't a natural winger and always felt more comfortable around the action. However, I was proud to do the job for my country. This was another opportunity and I was determined to impress.

At some stage during the first half, the French right-back received the ball from his goalkeeper on their right-wing about twenty-five yards out. Normally, or certainly, as I was used to playing, the center-forward would look to chase down the fullback. However, our centre-forward had decided to take a rest and wasn't chasing anyone. "Aaron Close him down, close him down" screamed an angry Maurice Setters from the dugout, situated about 20 yards behind me. Knowing that if I closed down the fullback on my own He'd play around me easily, I held my position and in doing so, kept our defensive unit solid. "I said close him down" screamed a furious Maurice Setters. As I continued to hold my ground, the full-back having no pass to make, turned around and played the ball back to his goalkeeper. I had ignored the yells from the bench but my actions were justified due to the result of my play. I had made the right choice. Little did I know what was facing me in the dressing room at half-time? The score was 0 - 0 and Setters stormed into the room. With an aggressive point of his finger toward me he growled "You off". His manner suggested that I had purposely done something outrageous on the pitch, something that had totally ruined our chances of success. It was like getting a kick in the lower regions. Here I was representing my country to the best of my ability, running and chasing like my life depended on it and this guy was gesturing to me like I cared less. As my anger boiled I kept my mouth shut but I was seething inside.

"When I tell you to do something, you do it" he bellowed out in my direction. This was too much, shaking with anger I spat back "They passed back to the goalkee—"Before I could finish I was face to face with Setters and the two of us were in a full-scale argument. It was a moment of pure rage and frustration on my part and although it only lasted a few seconds, it felt like a lifetime. I thoroughly understood that by doing what I was doing I was literally finishing my international prospects but the principal was too strong and I couldn't just lay down and let this guy do this.

As the row rolled on, I noticed Niall Quinn and a couple of other lads behind Setters miming "Sit down, sit down". The frenzy that I had worked myself into wasn't going anywhere and taking their advice, I retreated to my seat, still shaking with anger. As the team and Setters Went out for the second half, I sat there distraught "This is bad" I thought to myself. Eddie Corcoran who was part of the Irish entourage stayed behind. Shaking his head, he said, "Aaron, you've got to apologise after the game, I'm telling you now, you have to apologise". It was Eddie's only advice as he walked out the door. I knew he was right, although it was totally against my principles to do so.

With the game won and finished and the lads getting changed in the dressing room, I approached the man that I had felt like swinging at only 45 minutes before and apologised, hoping that too much damage hadn't been done. Maurice accepted the apology and said it was forgotten but I had to follow his instructions, as he was the coach. As I made my way towards the b us, one of the high-profile players tauntingly remarked "Kiss goodbye to your international career, you've got no chance now".

This was the night before we returned home and that evening we all went out and partied in Toulon. In fact, as virtually the entire team danced and sang atop a Toulon bar's tables, the anger of the earlier experience passed a little. Niall Quinn made me feel a lot better when he said "Don't mind what the others say, you play a few first-team games at your club, have a good run and they won't be able to leave you out of the international setup". They were comforting words and I always appreciated Niall's support unlike certain others. The night was a huge success and the next morning we were faced with an unhappy Maurice Setters. Some of the lads had raided the Hotel kitchen during the high-spirited previous evening. That was bad enough but Ricky Mc Evoy, a fantastic character particularly after a few drinks, had allegedly thrown a massive cake in the outdoor swimming pool.

Maurice calmly but assertively asked who had thrown the cake in the pool. As everyone sat with lips sealed like school kids in front of the headmaster, Niall knowing that he wouldn't be scolded said that he did it. He was right Maurice said nothing and that was the end of it. As we sat for breakfast the pool was emptied.

Although I feared I had done some damage to my immediate international prospects, I believed in what Niall had said. I still believed that fate was leading me toward a successful league and international career. Little did I know that I had in fact played my last game for Ireland? Looking back it was a sad way to finish my time with Ireland and to be honest I haven't ever thought of it that way until now. However, the Liam Brady experience and the pure proud feeling that you get when you l ine up for your country overpowers any bad feelings that I experienced. Ireland went on to have a hugely successful 1990 World Cup in Italy. For a very small time, I had been part of the entourage!

WHEN LOVE COMES TO TOWN

"I always long to see her yet we're never apart"

— Aaron Tighe "Blessing in Disguise" Copyright©
1991

Like all young men around the age of 19, it was important for me to have a social life as well as a professional career. At some stage, probably around the age of 16/17 our coach John Faulkener encouraged my parents to get me to go out with the lads and enjoy myself just like any other teenager. Although I would go out and just have an orange juice or a coke I would still get into the crack with the guys at the local pubs like the Moat House or the Warden Tavern. Mick Mickser Obrien, Ken Gilly Gillard, Alan Sully Osullivan, Paul Stumpy Grey, Jason Reecy Reece, and Gary Cobby Cobb were the usual crew I'd hang with amongst others and we had a good laugh together. Despite the pub environment beer for some reason just wasn't an attraction for me, much to the dismay of my mates who couldn't get enough. The pub visits were followed by dancing away or just standing watching in the nightclubs on a Saturday night. Like all guys, we would try to chat up girls and have a good laugh watching the failed attempts of our mates. Stick would fly between us and you had to be up for the challenge not only of impressing a lass but also of facing your mates if you got turned down. A whole night's conversation and banter would rely on such an incident.

As I just turned 20 years old in 1989 it was whilst drinking with the lads in the 'Moat Hose', a quaint local old Tudor-style pub that we saw a girl we knew by the name of Lara walk into the pub's lounge area with a stunning dark haired friend who I had never seen before. As we sat bunched around two tables Mick said what we were all thinking, "She's a fine bird". All eyes followed the girls, as they walked to the bar to order drinks. My gaze never left this new girl, there was instant attraction, who was she I wondered? To my delight, the girls purchased their drinks and made their way over towards where we were sitting finally sitting at a table adjacent to where I was sitting and more importantly for me shielded from the other lads. After a few minutes, turning my back on the lads, I bravely shuffled over to a free chair at the girl's table with just one thing on my mind, 'get to know that girl'. "Hi Lara I said, how are ya". I had become acquainted to Lara through one of the lad's girlfriends and happily started chatting to Lara who of course introduced me to 'the girl' named Julie. Deliberately I put on my best charm and set out on finding out as much as I could about her without being too intrusive. I found out importantly that Julie was a local girl who lived in Graham Gardens and that her surname was Meehan. It was all I needed. The plan was in place. Continuing to use all the charm that I could muster I set out to impress Julie, despite getting punches in the back from the lads who were obviously having a good laugh at my expense. Hoping that I had done enough to make an impression I bid farewell and silently took delight in the wonderful feeling that had entered my belly.

Nervously the next day I carried out my plan and eagerly searched diligently through the Luton and Dunstable phone book, discovering the Meehan name beside Graham Gardens. Hesitantly I picked up the phone "Hello is that Julie" "Yes" came the reply

"It's Aaron, I was talking to you in the pub last night, would you like to come out for a drink with me?" To my absolute joy, she agreed. Julie from that moment on became the most nerve-tingling, exciting, precious love of my life. I had met my wife-to-be, a true blessing, an angel sent from heaven.

THE FIRST TEAM CALLS

I arrived for the 1989/90 - pre-season f itter than I had ever been. Throughout the summer break, I made sure that I was in pristine condition. I was now signed on a new 3-year professional contract with a top-flight club and the opportunity was sure to arrive. When a manager offers a player a three- year contract he must justify his decision and that means playing you in the first team.

Luton at this time was a club who were on the edge of a precipice. Dave Evans the chairman at the time, a self-made millionaire who later went on to become an MP, had pumped money into the club but had left after the League Cup victory, and his financial backing departed also. Businessman David Kohler and a partner had taken over and Mr Kohler was ambitious and appeared to want to integrate with the playing staff, having his own training kit with D.K. sewn on for example. Unfortunately for Luton however after Mr Kohler's partner pulled out it appeared the club didn't have the financial muscle to support a top-flight billing as immediately top players began to leave the club. Internationals like Mick Harford to Derby (although he would return), Ricky Hill , Ashley Grimes and Brian Stein tofrance and Mal Donaghy to Manchester United.

Aaron Tighe

Goalkeeper Les Sealey was another who went to Man Utd, initially on loan but eventually as a star performer in United's European Cup Winners Cup victory and FA Cup final success around this time. It was a total clear out of the old guard and obviously the major wage earners.

The good news for me was that senior players leaving made it easier for me to break through to the first team. All I had to do was stay fit and I was confident it would happen. Pre-season got underway and despite my high levels of fitness a week or so into the intensive training, the unthinkable happened as I struck a ball during a typical training session. My dreaded left thigh muscle snapped, leaving me in a heap on the ground. As I lay on the ground I knew full well that this would severely halt my progress and put pay to any chance of me challenging for a first-team place in the near future. Before the season had even begun I was out of the picture, literally.

During every pre-season, professional clubs have a photo shoot to promote their squads and introduce their players to the public. Luton always carried theirs out on the plastic pitch at the main ground Kenilworth Road with one of the stands as the backdrop. This year my heart truly sank with disappointment when I wasn't included in the first team squad picture by Manager Ray Harford. Despite my injury, I had just signed a 3-year contract and was dismayed not to be included. This was made worse when my good friend Mickser O'Brien was included, as Mick lik e me had just signed a 3-year deal. Anyway, the show had to go on no matter how I felt.

By this time I was very familiar with a treatment routine for my thigh muscles. Both legs were giving me problems, but the left thigh was particularly weak. Battling in the gym and using the physio Dave Galleys' equipment and advice as much as possible, I got myself into match condition during the first month of the season. Despite the delay from my injury, I was soon performing well in reserve games and excitingly was becoming more and more involved with the first team training sessions. I must have continued to impress at this time as quite quickly I became a regular member of the first-team squad for training sessions and home and away first-team matches. I had finally moved out of the away team dressing room and had my own hanger in the first team dressing room. To my delight, I was also included in an updated first-team squad official photograph, which I distributed eagerly to family and friends. I recall visiting my old Tymon Bawn manager Noel Cummins's sports shop in Dublin sometime later and seeing the autographed team photo hung proudly on his wall, a nice feeling. My dream of playing first-team football was getting closer. It was just a matter of being patient. Working hard on my fitness in the gym, I did everything possible to ensure that my thigh muscles would hold up, I was on the way.

I can recall at this time that the more I trained with the first team the more confident I felt in my ability to compete against the first team lads, people like Captain Danny Wilson, an experienced terrier-like midfielder, who has since had a successful career in management, David Preece, another experienced player and an England B international, Roy Wegerle an American International, Lars Elstrup a Danish international who won a European Championship medal with Denmark, Mick Kennedy, a well known hard man of football and Irish international, Kingsley Black another Irish international and Richard Cooke, a quick right winger who had previously been with Tottenham, Iandowie, a dedicated aggressive Northern Ireland international, signed from non-league Hendon and Tim Breacker an experienced powerful full-back who continued his successful pro career at West Ham. Add to that list people like England's Mick Harford, Man Utd's and Northern Irelands' most capped player Mal Donaghy who had returned on loan along with excellent young players like Richard Harvey and Marvin Johnson, and the talent at the club was still very high and competitive.

Aaron Tighe

Being involved in the first-team squad was a terrific feeling for me but as the first team began to struggle at the bottom of the 1st Division, what is now the Premier League, I was growing impatient to break through. The first team coach at the time was a well-known ex-professional by the name of Terry Mancini. Terry was a nice guy and came across as one of the lads. Terry would continually say during training "I'm going to make you an international star son". It was a great way to give the young lads confidence but as the weeks of the season rolled on I still hadn't been included in the team. On one occasion we traveled to Everton for a League Cup fixture. Luton had only lost once in two seasons of League Cup fixtures and that was the previous season's final against Brian Cloughs Nottingham Forest. Everton was no longer the force that they had been in the mid-eighties and although an away fixture, Luton was confident of making it a stern contest. After some good training performances, I was hopeful of at least being included on the bench but was once again disappointed to be left out. Luton went down 4 - 1 and the dressing room afterward was silent. Ray Harford the boss let rip "I don't know whether it's the plastic pitch or what but none of you young lads can tackle to save your lives". What he said was true, the plastic pitch at Luton encouraged you to be what I call a stand-up defender, sliding or going to the ground was difficult as you ripped your legs open on the harsh surface when skin came in contact despite wads of Vaseline on knees and elbows.

On another occasion during a league visit to the home of Manchester City, the ground I had picked the grass from for a souvenir as a boy, I was once again majorly disappointed to be left out of the team lineup. In the dressing room Terry Mancini came over to me and pulled me to one side "I can't believe it, me and Ray had you down as sub last night, he must have changed his mind this morning" he said. Terry had obviously seen the disappointment on my face. I had been included in the squad for quite some time but hadn't been given a chance. I also wondered whether Terry was trying to keep all the players happy pending a possible sacking of Ray Harford. The team was struggling and lacked any invention and the crowd were showing their impatience. Who knows what was going on all I knew was that I had to get my chance soon or I was about to burst.

Finally, finally my first team breakthrough eventually arrived on a cold floodlit night at Oxford United's Manor Ground. It was a Zenith data fixture and Stumpy and me were announced as substitutes in the hotel prior to us leaving for the ground. I couldn't hold in my excitement,

all the hard work was paying off I was going to get a chance. Before the game, Harford told us that we would definitely be playing at some stage and to be prepared. That wasn't going to be a problem; I was totally up for it. After plenty of warm-ups up and down the side of the pitch to show my eagerness, we got the call from the Boss "You're on". There was about 20 minutes to go in the game and Oxford was leading 1 - 0 so we had some work to do. My adrenaline was pumping mad as Mick Kennedy came off and I entered the Arena.

Thinking back this was an amazing moment for me. This was a moment that happened maybe once in a lifetime. This moment was the culmination of all of the hours and years of playing football on the Green in Banbury, in the streets and parks of Tallaght, the clubs of Ireland, the dreaded Dublin and International trials, the youth and reserve games in England, the rise from the disappointments of injuries to that point and the successes of my youth. At the time I was just thinking about doing a good job and concentrating on what I had to do but looking back what a moment for me!

I immediately slotted in comfortably to my left side of three-midfield role and began to make an instant impact on the game with my pass and move football. Ray Harford to his credit recognised that I was not a natural wide midfielder but more of a central player and adapted the team structure to accommodate me as we moved to a 4 - 3 - 3 formation. Not long after coming on we gained a corner and from the resulting kick Stumpy nipped in at the near post and directed a neat header into the back of the net to take the tie into extra time. The subs had made a difference by equalizing and taking the game to Oxford and that was making me feel 10 feet tall. In extra time we continued to control the game and took the lead. Apart from the feeling of turning the game around, I had the joy of receiving lots of the ball as I hunted it down in midfield and played like a man rather than a debutant. We held on comfortably to win the game and as I shook hands with former Luton heroes and now Oxford players Steve Foster and Mark Stein, I was truly thrilled right down to my boots. In the dressing room, I received plenty of pats on the back and hair ruffling from the Boss and Terry Mancini. "Some debut" said Kingsley Black excitedly. Kingsley the regular wide left player was injured at the time, so it meant a lot when he said that. It was an endorsement that I had proven myself. I went home a proud man.

That evening as I returned home to my parent's house on Swasedale Road Luton, we sat and talked about the game. My dad gave me a gold ring saying "We've been waiting to present this to you for ages; we got it for when you made your debut, well done son". Life was looking up, I had appeared to have gotten over my thigh injury, I had proved myself as a first-team player, and in my personal life was thoroughly in love with that beautiful girl Julie. My fate was being realised, I could feel it way down deep.

The next morning I had to report for training with Jim Ryan the reserve team coach. I can remember feeling that it was a total comedown to be training with the reserves after such a terrific night. The thing was that now I had tasted first-team football, it was all I wanted. Although I did the training as best as I could, I had to admit that my heart just wasn't in it, despite Jim's usual enthusiasm. I wanted every moment from now on to be first-team moments playing in front of a crowd and being successful.

To prove the roller-coaster ride of emotions as a footballer I was once again disappointed to not be included in the first 13 for the next league fixture after the Oxford game. I was perplexed at this decision after having such a good debut and no explanation was ever given when I was left out. Keeping my head down I got on with trying to impress it was all felt I could do. My next opportunity came in the next round of the Zenith data Cup. Luton were drawn against Crystal Palace away. On the day before the game Ray Harford took a session where we practiced our tactics using a session called shadow play. Shadow play is where you line up in your positions and play without opposition. It's a useful method for a coach to show how he wants you to play and what positions to take up. In this particular session, I scored a 30-yard cracker which whistled into the top corner past our goalkeeper Alec Chamberlain. I can still see Ray Harford's look of amazement at the strike. Inside I was saying "Just play me, Boss, I can handle this". It was obviously on his mind as I was slotted into a new 5 - 3 - 2 formation in my central left midfield position. I was definitely playing the following night. "Leo and Marie will be happy their son's making his debut," said Danny Wilson as we walked off the Luton plastic. Mum and Dad, particularly Mum had made friends with some of the senior player's wives, hence the comment from our Captain.

A young defender called Tim Allpress was also making his full debut the following night. Tim was a tall Alan Hansen type player with good touch and passing. Tim was lined up to play sweeper in a 3 man defense with Richard Harvey on the left and Tim Breacker as the other wing-back. David Preece was playing centre-midfield with me on the left and Danny Wilson on the right. Up front, we had the aggressive Iandowie and the talented Roy Wegerle. I can recall in the lead-up to the game that I was totally composed and confident. I knew I could handle myself and was thrilled at the prospect of starting in the first team. I roomed with Tim at a London Hotel on the day of the game and had no problem getting off to sleep for an afternoon nap in preparation for the game.

Crystal Palace at this time in 1989 was a strong team with players such as Ian Wright and Mark Bright up front. In midfield, they had Andy Gray and Geoff Thomas with Nigel Martyn in goal. They went on this season to play Manchester United in the FA Cup Final, which was no mean feat and shows the quality of the team. In the Selhurst Park dressing room and in the warm-up I prepared myself for the game in a manner that I made a habit of after my Leicester days. I splashed cold water on my face in the shower area, stretched, and did some knee to chest jumps, focusing totally on how I would play. Once on the pitch, I warmed up by, sharply receiving the ball, turning to open my body out and passing. It was a preparation for exactly what I expected to be doing in the game and a way to make sure I was as mentally prepared as possible.

The beginning of the game under the Selhurst Park floodlights was not played at a thunderous pace as I expected and I was pleasantly surprised by the feeling that there was nothing to be alarmed by. It was business as usual. About 15 minutes into the game Richard Harvey put over a terrific cross and Iandowie typically rose at the far post to steer an excellent header into the Palace net. 1 - 0 up and cruising, the game had a surreal feeling to it. We were simply too comfortable. Although I wasn't getting as much of the ball as I would have liked I was doing my job and felt comfortable. However as football tends to do, the unthinkable unraveled before my eyes. I can't quite recall which was first but one by one in the space of a crazy 5 minutes, my fellow midfielders, the experienced guys who had been given instructions to look after me, were sent off. In an appalling display of refereeing, one of the lads, I think it was Danny, was shown the red card for a mistimed tackle. Before we even regrouped Preecy was also shown the red card for talking back to the ref. To add to the debacle Terry Mancini our first team coach was also shown a red card as he remonstrated from the sidelines. I stood in the middle of the park looking towards a shocked Ray Harford thinking, "What do you want me to do now". There was still another twenty minutes or so left in the first half and we were down to 9 men. I was so angry at the situation that my adrenaline began to race and before I knew it I was racing from one side of the pitch to the other attempting to close down the Palace midfielders." Bizzy calm down, you'll knacker yourself," shouted our wing back Richard Harvey. He was right. Amazingly we defended stoutly and went into the dressing room at halftime 1 - 0 up. The Boss told us to keep the 5 at the back, play two in midfield, and just leave one up front, basically defending our penalty box for 45 minutes. "Aaron, Roy (wegerle), if either of you get the ball I just want you to run with it, take players on, commit them," said Ray as we made our way out for the challenging second half.

Palace as you would expect cruised the second half and even when we did get the ball, our lack of passing options meant they came straight back at us. The palace midfielder Andy Gray welcomed me to first-team football with a bludgeoning elbow as I pressured him from behind. "don't worry Dave, I'll be a hero", I jokingly said to physio Dave Galley as he attempted to stop the blood-pouring out of my nose. I was literally lying on the grass seeing nothing but stars. Whether it was adrenaline flowing or purely the hard physical work I was doing in training I felt as fit as I had ever done, chasing and defending the Palace players as they used the acres of space in our midfield area. We held out for a while before conceding 4 goals in a very disappointing result. "Well played Bizzy," said Jim Ryan in the dressing room afterward. I was thankful for his encouragement but failed to see how he thought I played well. I did chase and harry our opponents as best as I could, but had failed to get much of the ball, which was understandable given the circumstances. The boss also took me off with ten minutes or so to go "You were beginning to look tired son" he said. This was probably true given the amount of work I had put in but I would have liked to have seen it through to the end. Despite the disappointment of the result at Palace, I still enjoyed the feeling of being part of the first team and was even keener to make more regular appearances.

However, fate, which I had trusted implicitly, dealt me a cruel blow.

A few days later after a tough morning session with the first team which involved short sharp running drills called "doggies", I was relaxing with a few of the younger lads in the Home team dressing room, when Jim Ryan the reserve team manager came in. "Lads I'm taking the reserves and the apprentices up to the running track to work on sprinting, any of you want to come?" asked Jim. Although I should have had the sense to say 'no' due to heavy legs from the morning session, I had always been one who was totally committed to being a 'dedicated player'. Although I didn't feel like going, I agreed to do the extra work. At the rugby club running track, despite my usual thorough warm-up, I began to experience a sharp pain in my right groin. Stupidly I carried on finishing the session, hoping that it was just one of those tweaks that happen now and again. Over the next few days, I trained with the first team as normal, hiding as best as I could the injury, which was gradually getting worse.

I was keen to impress in training based on an opportunity to be selected to play at Arsenal for a first-team evening fixture. I was optimistic that I would be picked for the game and mentally was dismissing the groin injury, which hadn't been put to the test in a game situation. To my annoyance and puzzlement, although a good decision due to my secret injury, I was left out again. The boss decided to bring back an unfit Kingsley Black, whilst also playing veteran midfielder Steve Williams.

Although a tough decision for me for this game I had the utmost respect for Steve Williams. He was one of the most talented players I have ever seen or played with. He had previously carved out a very successful career with Southampton, Arsenal and

England. Steve was the most self-confident bloke I had ever come across and was not afraid to tell people who he was, particularly referees. During games, he would constantly cajole and wind up refs. On occasions when he was booked he would say "Ref you're only booking me because of who I am" or "You just want to tell your mates you've booked Steve Williams!" I clearly recall Steve's fantastic ability to shield the ball from defenders, whilst continuing to maneuver the ball at leisure, seeking out a pass. He also had this ability to disguise his passes, rarely looking in the direction where the pass would go. As a player, I learned to look at my opponents' eyes when they were on the ball to gauge where they were about to pass. It was amazing how often you would intercept a pass using that technique. However, with Steve, that was difficult, as you never knew where he was passing it. I learned so much about shielding and disguising passing from Steve during these seasons from working closely with him in training that it has always stuck with me and is something that I encourage now in my coaching drills with young players. Steve also helped me in games through encouragement with things like passing me a ball and immediately I'd hear "Go on take him on Bizzy, you'll do him", great confidence-boosting words.

Another member of the Luton side facing Arsenal that evening was Mal Donaghy. Mal who I believe is the most capped Irish international, had just before the Arsenal game returned to Luton on loan from Manchester United. Mal was a terrific guy and as we sat on the team bus I probably bored him to death with questions about United. Despite Mal's return and Steve Williams getting a standing ovation from the Highbury crowd where he was obviously very well thought of in his playing days, Luton was well and truly beaten by Arsenal on the nights and the only good thing about the visit to Highbury was the chance to be in those special dressing rooms, where the tiles on the floor are heated, luxury or what! I always loved playing at grounds like Highbury, Upton Park, Stamford Bridge, and Tottenham's White Hart Lane, purely because of the history that was attached to those football clubs and the thoughts of the great players who had performed there. When on one occasion an ex-Arsenal player Ian Allinson crossed from the right and I half-volleyed a right foot shot past John Lukic into the net at Highbury, I was thrilled to bits even if it was only a reserve match!

During the training session following the Arsenal game, I was still hiding my groin injury. I nervously approached Ray Harford as training finished on the plastic at Kenilworth Road. "Boss can I have a word with you" "Sure son" came the reply" as we took a seat on a low wall surrounding the pitch. "I want to know why you didn't pick me for the Arsenal game?" Ray went on to explain that he took a risk with Kingsley due to wanting to play his most experienced players but in hindsight had made a mistake and should have played me. The fact that he had said this put me in a strong position for the upcoming fixtures but first there was a reserve game to attend to.

The plastic pitch was pretty unforgiving if you had an injury and in my case, the groin injury which had been hidden during training, showed in the first half. "Are you injured cause you look injured, you can't run?" enquired the Boss at half time. "Yes, Boss" was the only reply I could muster. With that, I was subbed and welcomed back to the treatment room by physio Dave Galley. Just as things were hotting up for first-team opportunities I found myself frustratingly out of the action again, the timing couldn't have been worse, and little did I know the impact this groin injury would have on my career. Shortly after the reserve game the news filtered through that the pressure of poor results had got to the Board and that Ray Harford had been given sacked. Poor performances by the players and the quoted suggestion by a director that he didn't smile a lot led to his dismissal? Despite his success as the only manager who had lifted a major trophy with Luton. I had mixed feelings about Ray leaving. He had given me a 3-year contract and my first team debut. On the other hand, I was still only a squad player and felt I should have had more opportunities, hard to call what was best for my career.

Terry Mancini Ray's assistant was placed in temporary charge of the team whilst the Board decided who would take over. A couple of days before an FA Cup fixture at Brighton, Terry asked me if I would be fit for the game as he was looking to play me. Painfully I had to say 'no' as my groin wouldn't allow me to run at any pace. My mate Jason Reece played instead and went from strength to strength from that game on. Unfortunately for Terry, the game was dismally lost at Brighton and more dismally I had lost my chance to impress.

Although various big names were banded about for the vacant manager's role the club quickly announced that the new manager was to be reserve team manager Jim Ryan, which surprised a number of people, but was down to the fact that Jim had produced outstanding attractive flowing football from us lads at reserve level. In a packed home team dressing room our new Boss gave an inspirational speech, pointing out that whether or not he had the respect of the senior players, the fact was, that everyone at the club was bottom of the league, and unless everyone at the club pulled together, everyone would be division two players the following season. I remember leaving the room really revved up and totally impressed with Jim's approach to stepping up to the mark.

Jim's main philosophy in football was team spirit. A team that has true team spirit is very hard to beat. I can recall him preaching, "If one of our lads is in a scuffle, I don't want him to be on his own, let them know that we're a team". To back this up Jim as reserve team manager acquired a punch bag, which was hung up in the gym. He then got a local boxing trainer to come in and give us a lesson on how to fight. It was all a bit of a laugh but was an excellent way to show us that we had to be tough to survive out there. It all helped to build a team spirit. That spirit would help Luton Town, with little or no money, survive in the top flight under Jim Ryan, by winning the last game of the season two years on the trot, now that's spirit under pressure!

After a couple of attempted comebacks over a number of weeks, the groin injury was worse than ever. During that season there had been a whole spate of Luton players receiving hernia operations by the famous Harley Street surgeon Dr. Gilmore. It was almost an epidemic with something like 9 players receiving the op. I remember chatting to Dave Galley during a typical spell of treatment in the medical room and Dave was asking me what I thought was causing the injuries. It was a choice between the plastic pitch, the balls we were using, or the type of physical training we were doing, particularly in the Gym using weights. We never did identify the cause but in my case, it had been an overworked muscle.

As my injury wasn't getting better and I was suffering from hernia-type symptoms, myself and Paul Telfer a young pro and one of the most naturally fit people I have met (he would later go on to have a very successful career at Coventry, Southampton, and Celtic), visited Dr. Gilmore in Harley St. After Telf had been examined and was given the thumbs up, it was my turn on the treatment table. As I lay there on the table Mr. Gilmore using his very big little finger, thrust it into a hole in my scrotum somewhere, which made me literally jump 5 feet in the air with the pain. As I landed with his big little finger still lodged in my lower abdomen, he asked the impossible "Now cough", from the deep reaches of my throat I let out a cough come scream. While I lay in agony on the bench Gilmore turned to Dave Galley "We will need to operate". It was bad news but at least we knew the problem and could do something about it, the weeks leading up to this point had been frustrating to the extreme as I saw young lads being given the opportunity to impress in the first team under Jim. All I could do was watch on as my chance went to others.

The expected time out after the operation was 6 weeks, which didn't make my chances of getting back in the first team reckoning very good, but I had no choice. The operation at London's wonderful Princes Grace Hospital went well and the second day after the op, I was doing walking exercises to help prevent the build-up of scar tissue. I remember that getting out of bed to go to the toilet was like climbing a mountain and on one occasion, I fainted and woke up on the hospital room floor being told emphatically by my nurse "It told you to call me, if you needed help!" The next day I had just made the arduous 5-minute 4-metre journey to the bathroom when in my crouched-over position I was suddenly pinched on the bum. The fright made me hit the ceiling and I turned to see a worried Julie saying "Sorry, sorry I didn't mean it, I forgot". Julie had made the long journey into the hospital from Luton, once with my Mum and then bravely on her own. It was great to see her. As I departed the hospital my hero Bryan Robson came in for the same operation and I remember thinking to myself, if he can recover so can I. The recovery went according to plan and after six weeks I was playing football again but by this stage, the season was drawing to a close and I was a long way from my earlier season form. My fitness had suffered and I recall having a chat with temporary reserve manager Les Shannon explaining that I felt unfit and couldn't cover the ground. "you'd be surprised at how f it you are Aaron," said Les "Maybe it's just in your head". However, I knew the difference between how I had felt prior to the groin injury and how I felt at the tail end of the season and the difference was vast.

After some heroics by the first-team lads away at Derby County on the last day of the season, we avoided relegation. To stay up Luton was required to win away and Ron Atkinson's Sheffield Wednesday had to lose at home. Luton won 3 - 2 on the day and Sheffield was beaten. Most of the lads who weren't playing went up to the game to add their support; I had sulkily stayed in Luton and watched the result come through on the television. I was delighted that the team had won but had mixed feelings due to my non-involvement in the game and my own personal disastrous second half of the season. What should have been my year was punctuated by my first excitement at being involved with the first team and making my debut, followed by the hernia injury and then disappointedly continued problems with my thigh strains towards the end of the year. I had begun to feel like an outsider with the first team squad as it had been a good 5 months since I was involved and my confidence was obviously shaken. Probably recognizing this, before we wound up for the season, Jim Ryan called me into his office. As Jim was now the Boss, his manner as you would expect, had become more authoritative. "Aaron would you like to come on the end-of-season trip to Marbella with the first team" "I'd love to" I replied, "It was between you and Ceri Hughes but because you were involved in the first team for longer, you got the nod". The closing remark was a reminder that I was only included due to my early season form. A number of younger players including Welsh midfielder Ceri Hughes had broken into the team ahead of the constantly injured Aaron Tighe. This was a lifeline from the Boss, saying 'You're still in our thoughts but only just'. Due to the long period that I had been away from the first team, the trip was never comfortable for me. I no longer felt that I fitted in, which was a strange feeling. Also after Jim's remarks, I didn't like the idea that 'I was lucky to be involved'. The week away at a remote Hotel in Marbella on Spain's southern coast was purely a holiday. The weather ended up being awful and we found ourselves looking for things to do. The highlight was a night out at the beautiful Porto Benous, a wonderful salubrious harbour with yachts so big that one had a helicopter perched on it. By coincidence, the Sheffield Wednesday players were also there that night, with no ill feelings, despite Luton putting them down. The trip due to the bad weather was one of those where you were waiting to go back home, apart from a couple of the senior players who weren't seen for the entire week after finding some girlfriends!

TWO HOMES

1990/91

The summer of 1990 began with optimism and hope. Hope is the first building block of motivation and I was praying that my thigh injuries would prevail to allow me to compete for a first-team place in a mediocre first team. Jim Ryan was still in place as manager with former youth team coach John Faulkener as his assistant. John Moore was welcomed back as reserve team coach. They were all coaches whom I had worked with closely through my teenage years and who recognised my ability. My mission was simple. Get myself fit and play well. The summer had seen the departure of my good Dublin friend Neil Poutch. Poutchy had made it into the first team at the end of the season but unfortunately didn't have his contract renewed. It brought home to me how precarious our position was as professional footballers.

On the personal front, I had bought my first house at Marsom Grove Luton, a modern two-bedroomed end of terrace, situated on the northern outskirts of the town. Mum and Dad had decided to go back to Dublin. It was the right time as I was twenty years old and ready for my independence. The fact that I lived in my own place helped me grow up a bit, something that was significantly needed in the coming year. After a few months, I asked Julie to move in with me, which made sense, as she was more with me than she was at home. Julie at the time was a ground stewardess with Monarch Airlines at Luton airport and her shift-like hours of work fitted in well with my football lifestyle. Outside of football, you couldn't have found a happier man, as our love for each other grew stronger than ever.

My other home for the year was the Luton Town medical room. Painfully, during pre-season, my thigh muscle broke down again. By this stage, I had ruptured and strained my thigh muscles so many times, that the instant it happened I literally hung my head and accepted the fact that I would be out for at least 4 weeks. Each time the injury occurred, it felt like my chances of making it back to the first team were becoming more distant.

Matters got worse when my left thigh, in particular, kept on breaking down putting me out of action for months at a time. Our physio Dave Galley couldn't get to grips with the injury despite trying a mixture of physical work combined with laser treatment etc. Blood tests were taken and the Club doctor ran a check but no solutions were found. Months into the new season Aaron Tighe had hardly kicked a ball.

It was decided that I should go to a Sports injury clinic in Chiswick London until fully recovered. Dave's mate was a physio there and they had the latest Cybex equipment, a terrific machine that measures the strengths and weaknesses of muscles in graphical form. I was in for a shock. On arrival at the clinic, which was a top-notch health club with social facilities and excellent amenities, I introduced myself to Martin, Dave's mate. He wasted no time in telling me that I would be expected to work very hard while I was there. They would give me a program to work in and it would be up to me to follow it if I wanted success.

After an initial warm-up, I was introduced to the Cybex machine. As I sat in the chair and Martin strapped my ankles to the protruding metal legs, which were resting peacefully a foot away from the floor, I had no idea what to expect. Martin went on to explain that, the machine would put me through a program of tests where it would provide resistance against me as I kicked upwards using my quadriceps muscles and then pulled downwards using my hamstrings. He then went on to show me the type of colourful charts that the linked up computer would produce. It all sounded great but then we started to work. After a few easy practice runs to get used to it and warm up, we launched into the session. Martin's snarling blasts of "harder. faster, come on, come on" said it all. The machine smoothly imitated the resistance of a tonne of bricks and my muscles screamed with 'please stop, please stop'. I gave it all I had for the 15-minute or so session and was expecting to be announced as one of the best performers the machine had ever come up against. I was in for a surprise! As Martin pulled off the chart readings and showed them to me, he said, "This is your problem, Aaron. The women that I have in here have stronger thigh muscles than you. You can see that at the beginning and end of the chart, your strength at these stages is appalling but in the middle of the session it's not too bad, that's due to the amount of scar tissue that you have in your thighs which can't react quickly like a regular muscle" He went on to explain that scar tissue isn't flexible and doesn't stretch easily and had built up as a replacement for the damaged tissue whenever a rupture or tear occurred. The quadricep muscle needs to stretch very quickly when kicking a ball and this was the problem. Next came the bombshell "This injury may finish your career and you should be aware of that" Martin said. Talk about a moment in your life when time stands still, this was it and the words will stick with me forever. I had never thought for a moment that my career as a professional footballer was in jeopardy. The words sunk in but I didn't believe them. Martin carried on explaining that it would take an enormous amount of effort and work to build up the muscles and break down the scarring in my thighs. He also suggested as a last resort an operation to remove the scar tissue but this was a last resort as more scarring may be created when opened up. It was a scary conversation and I was prepared to jump through hoops to prevent a disastrous outcome.

Martin set out a full day's program of weight training, swimming, hopping, and bike work, targeted at strengthening my badly damaged quadricep muscles. The following morning I swear, I couldn't get out of bed. As a professional footballer, I had been used to hard physical punishing work but had never felt as stiff as this. Somehow I managed to force myself down to London. "Martin" I explained, "My thighs are so stiff I'm scared to do anything today". His reply was simple "Well, if we're gonna do some damage, let's do it now, make sure you warm up properly and do it all again, it's vital we get rid of that scarring" Amazingly enough, the legs held out and after a couple of days the stiffness passed and I found myself improving in strength. After 2 weeks I was buzzing and felt ready to give it a test.

At the end of the two weeks I had the pleasure, with mixed emotions, to watch enthralled as one of the greatest Athletes ever, Daly Thompson, was put through his paces on the Cybex machine. Daly was coming to the end of his athletics career at the time but was still an awesome display of power, as he kicked and pulled with all his might. The reason for the mixed emotions was that although it was great to see him in action, I had to get on the chair immediately after him and that was scary! Despite my fears, the test on the machine was positive. The results showed an enormous improvement in my muscle strength and Martin gave me the thumbs up to return to Luton for training, using the first couple of days to test striking a football. I could do all the weights, hopping, swimming, and running in the world but until I kicked a ball a few times I wouldn't know if I was ready.

The tests with the ball although tentative initially, were positive and I came through unscathed. My legs felt stronger than ever and my overall fitness levels appeared to have improved. It was time to join in training with the lads. After months on the sideline, it's a strange feeling when you join in with the lads. You get a little buzz feeling but at the same time a scared feeling that things could go wrong again. You're basically at a crossroads waiting to see what will happen. The first training session took place at our Houghton Regis training ground and I found myself settling back in nicely and enjoying a practice match between the youth and reserve team players. As my confidence grew the injury was forgotten and I was playing with a free mind. One of my attributes as a player was timing forward runs from midfield and on this occasion as I sprinted in behind two defenders, Darren Macdonough played an accurate high ball from deep, which glided its way over my head. Still sprinting I raised my left foot to catch the ball before it bounced and suddenly 'Bang'. As if I had been shot by a gun my left thigh muscle snapped. As the coach John Faulkener helped carry me off the pitch, Martin's words were foremost in my mind "This injury may finish your career". My heart sank at the thought of what lay ahead.

The following few weeks were spent back down in Chiswick London. The rehabilitation program resumed until once again I was given the all-clear. At least this time, I would resume playing for a couple of months. These months would be followed by sporadic muscle tears, which would limit the games played. During an away Reserve match at Carrow Road Norwich, I lined up with talented midfielder Paul Holsgrove in my favourite centre-midfield position. I had been fit for a reasonable period of time and wanted to perform well in front of manager Jimmy Ryan. I had a terrific game hitting the bar with a long-range effort and forcing the goalkeeper into some excellent saves. Jim remarked on how well I had played after the game and I had shown that my game was almost back to its best, a couple more similar performances were likely to push me back into the first team. However the following day at training, the injury struck again and once again I was sidelined for a long period.

Aaron Tighe

The second year of my three-year contract, to put it bluntly, was a disaster. The limited playing time didn't allow me to perform anywhere near my best consistently and my confidence had been put to the test. Just when I was building up some momentum, the thigh injury would strike. I also found that some games I did take part in were passing me by. I had all the intentions of playing fantastically well but as things didn't go right I felt myself becoming a passenger of the game rather than an instigator or a playmaker. I once read an interview with the world champion fighter Lloyd Honeygan. The interview took place after he had lost a fight and he explained how he could feel the fight going away from him but helplessly let it carry on. It wasn't that he wanted to lose but he simply felt like a spectator rather than a participant, a recipe for disaster. The truth was that I was a long way from where I wanted to be and unless I could remain fit the following season would be my last. I was approaching my 22nd birthday in July and how long can a Football club hold on to a constantly unfit player?

Luton once again survived the drop to the old second division on the last day of the season. This time it was a home game against Derby County, where ex-Luton man Mick Harford, luckily for Luton, scored an unintentional own goal in his typical headed fashion. In a twist of fate in the close season, Mick then returned to Kenilworth Road as a player. Mick had to be the best target man I have ever seen in person. He had a wonderful touch on the ball combined with an awesome aerial ability. He sometimes would ask me to knock over crosses for him after training. As I'd pitch the ball high towards the penalty spot, He'd rise and hang in the air before bulleting a header into the empty net, a truly awesome sight. Alex Ferguson the Manchester United manager claims in his autobiography, that he should have signed Mick back in 1991 and it was a major mistake not doing so. I'd agree, but Mick should have been playing for Manchester Utd a lot sooner than that.

Despite Luton's miracle escape from the jaws of relegation once again, Jim Ryan was unthinkably sacked at the end of the 90/91 season. It was a typical example of a Board or executive being totally out of touch with what was happening on the playing side. There was talk at the time that Jim had been given an ultimatum to reduce the playing staff numbers and had failed to do so. The fact that he had kept the club in the top flight against all the odds however had counted for nothing. Jim was snapped up immediately by Manchester United as reserve team coach and went on to help develop the magnificent Man Utd youngsters of the nineties and become a valuable member of Alex Fergusons' coaching team. The funny thing is, Jim loved Manchester United and really fell on his feet. The same couldn't be said for Luton, whose lack of finance would lead to disaster.

PLEAT RETURNS

Jim's replacement was David Pleat. When I first heard the news, my heart skipped a beat in anticipation. Pleat had been an admirer of my football since I was a kid, once again all I had to do was stay fit and I would have a great chance. My hope had returned.

During the close season Julie and I set off on a fantastic holiday to Los Angeles. Julie, being a stewardess with Monarch Airlines, managed to purchase flights for 25 pounds each, what a bargain! On arrival, we picked up a car rental, with no map to guide us, and set off for our Hotel which was situated in downtown LA. After driving on the wrong side of the road a few times and having no idea of where we were, we eventually followed a taxi to our destination. At the time we had no idea that Downtown LA isn't exactly a holiday resort but our hotel was fine. Every day we set off for different tourist attractions like Disneyland, Venice Beach, Santa Monica, Magic Mountain, and Hollywood. It was great to put my worries behind me and for two weeks I was totally relaxed. I remember saying to Julie one day on the beach "Pleat loves me, this is the break I've been waiting for" On another day whilst strolling down Venice beach, Julie pulled a reluctant Aaron over to a Tarot card reader to have our fortune told. "There will be a major change in direction in your life" the woman said, she wasn't wrong!

After a magical time in LA, I headed off to Ireland for a week or so. It was there that I took the biggest kick in the **** imaginable. Over a cup of tea in the dining room of my Mum and Dad's house in Tallaght, my Dad explained that David Pleat had called while I was in LA and had told him that I didn't figure in his plans. He told my Dad that he would be looking to offload me as soon as I returned for pre-season. The words hit me like a bombshell. It was totally unexpected and I was fuming that firstly he hadn't spoken to me and secondly he wasn't even going to give me a chance. I saw my entire career flash before my eyes, all the work, all the effort, all the sacrifice, and all of my dreams since I was a toddler on 'the Banbury green'. There were still a few weeks to pre-season but I had to confront David Pleat before then.

After a hasty return to Luton, I arranged a meeting with the manager. I remember an hour or so before I was due to meet him, I was walking through the town centre and my legs were shaking with nerves. I had experienced nerves before but never to this extent, I was literally shaking and there was still plenty of time before I met the man who said he would end my seven-year relationship with a top-flight professional football club. When the meeting finally took place inside Luton's Kenilworth Road Ground I felt like a little boy who had been sent to the school's Headmaster and my nerves were just being kept under control. As Pleat sat behind his desk, eating a bread roll and some soup, we discussed my position. I recall finding that incredibly rude that here he was trying to end my lifelong ambition, whilst at the same time eating his soup. I mean, I understand that he was a busy man but still............ At the time I felt anger building up inside at the situation but still being a little frightened kept it at bay.

"I saw you play a reserve match at Millwall last season and you're not half the player you were," he said to me. Quickly and defensively I responded with "I had just come back from injury at the time, that's why" I followed on by explaining the injury problems that I had been having but that I had another year on my contract and I was determined to stay f it and prove myself. Pleat remarked "I'm warning you now, I'm going to make it very difficult for you here, I have too many players and there are a few ahead of you like Mark Pembridge and Ceri Hughes, it must have been demoralising seeing them come through ahead of you!" he said. The words stung as he had hit a nerve. He was right; it had been hard watching younger players who I was ahead of leapfrog over me. The man knew how to hit you. "Boss, I'm not going anywhere and I'll prove myself," I said. As I left his office, my world was a very dark place and the pressure was truly crushing.

With two weeks to go before pre-season got underway, Julie suggested that we should take another holiday and get away. It was a great idea and having only a little bit of money left, we packed our bags and headed up to Luton airport, only knowing that we wanted to get away from the pressure and run off somewhere to the sunshine. As we looked up the various flights on the Luton Airport departure board and chose Spain's wonderful Mallorca, the thought of a few more days' break felt good. On arrival at Mallorca we hopped on one of the tour buses and ended up in the beautiful Santa Ponsa, a small town on the south side of the island. The week helped ease my fears and gave me time to build up my determination. Julie was fantastic as ever and the two of us enjoyed a wonderful week together.

Aaron Tighe

Whilst in Mallorca and on my return to Luton I made sure that my fitness levels were brought up to spec in preparation for the battle that was about to begin. Every day I'd go into the club and work on running, gym work, and completing the hardest level on the bike machine for 12 minutes, which really increased the power in my legs. I was ready to defend myself against the loss of my dreams. Somewhere inside I was still convinced being a successful footballer was my fate, despite the injury problems that had been occurring for over 4 years and despite the insistence from my Boss that I would be leaving.

"LET THE BROKEN HEARTS STAND AS THE PRICE YOU GOTTA PAY"

B. Springsteen

Pre season got underway and with both Jimmy Ryan and his assistant John Faulkener gone, David Pleat brought in Colin Murphy as his assistant coach along with a young youth coach by the name of Terry Westley. The youth team hadn't reached great heights since our successful team of a few years earlier and improvement was needed. A gangly young Welsh lad by the name of John Hartson also arrived at the club as an apprentice and despite being consistently last in the long-distance running, would go on to become a very successful premier league centre-forward, which reminds me of the beauty of the sport. What you lack in one area can be made up in other areas of your game. Johnny certainly proved that as he went from one multi-million pound deal to another. I can recall having a conversation with coach Terry Westley and him saying that John was going to be a real star. Boy was he right.

One of the surprises in the new coaching team was Colin Murphy the new first-team coach. He was definitely one of the most unusual characters I had ever met in the game. Colin was a likable guy who looked a bit like Phil Collins the singer and like a true performer who employed some strange techniques in training. One of his favourites during the warm-up was to get everyone lying on the ground. You'd then hear him shouting "Lets hear you laugh, I want to hear you laugh" If somebody didn't laugh he'd run over to them, put his face right in front of theirs, and carry on screaming "laugh, c'mon laugh". I never really got it, you know? I think everyone was a little bit stunned when he did it, because it was so off the wall. Colin was a decent guy and obviously knew how to coach but I didn't get too much work time with him and the likes of John Moore, Jimmy Ryan, and John Faulkener who articulated how to play the game in an attractive style had more of an impact on my game.

Terry Westley on the other hand immediately struck me as a professional coach. Although he worked only with the youth team, I was impressed by his manner and the sessions he put on for the young lads. A couple of years later I would complete my preliminary coaching badge with Terry and would learn a great deal from his lessons. Terry went on to take over as manager from David Pleat a few seasons later but unfortunately, only for a short time, a shame really as I felt he had a lot of ability and dedication. To this day while coaching kids I use the techniques he showed me.

During the pre-season period, the manager David Pleat made it blatantly clear whom he wanted to keep and who he wanted to get rid of from the club. One example of this that sticks in my mind was when football boots were being ordered for all the lads in the dressing room. Normally the kit man would carry out such a role but David Pleat the manager of the club took it upon himself to go around asking the boot size of the players in the dressing room. Failing to hear his name called, David Gormley, a lad who had just turned professional, asked "Boss you didn't mention me?" to which Pleat snapped "You won't be needing any boots here, son!" It was a cruel moment, as Pleat had said it for all to here in the dressing room. Some of the other lads, whose names hadn't been called, didn't dare to ask for fear of being embarrassed. The Boss certainly knew how to make you feel unwanted.

In my case, he did exactly what he said he would do in our initial meeting a few weeks earlier and made life very uncomfortable for me. He would do things like continually leaving me out of practice matches between the first team and reserves but then call me over, put me on for five minutes take me back off again, and leave me off for the remainder of the session. Other methods used to make me uncomfortable were making me train with the youth team or placing me as a sub in the reserve fixtures. On one occasion after a reserve match the night before and a full session the next morning, he pulled some of us to one side and ran us into the ground with shuttle runs. As we walked away exhausted towards the dressing rooms about 100-metres away, Pleat stoically screamed "Don't walk, sprint, sprint and everybody beat Tighe, beat Tighe, he doesn't want to win". A build-up of pressure had got to me at this stage and this was the final straw, my temper was boiling and I had to do something about it.

By this time pre-season games that I had taken part in had gone well despite the circumstances and harassment I was receiving. I had managed to play in my favourite centre-midfield position and found some excellent form. It was the first time since being an apprentice that I had stayed fit through pre-season and I was feeling the benefit. However, this wasn't making any impression on Pleat, and following the "beat Tighe embarrassment" I decided that I had to tell him what I thought. The following day I booked an appointment to see him at the club offices. I ran through in my mind exactly what I was going to say and with the rage still burning inside was determined to say my piece. The Boss made me wait for two hours in reception before telling the receptionist to send me up which got me even angrier, I mean two hours to leave someone sitting waiting for you, pushing it, or what! As I walked into Mr. Pleat's office my legs had begun the nervous shaking bit. He sat behind his big desk and beckoned me to sit down. Even before my bum had touched the seat I let r ip "Boss, I've just come to say that I've lost all respect for you as a man and as a manager, and that goes for my family too and the way you've been treating me is diabolical and—"The words carried on spilling out and no longer did I feel like a little boy but a man possessed. As I finished my tirade of words, he leaned back and said "I've been waiting for that but I think it's too late!"

At the time I never took in the words that he said to me. Now looking back I understand. Pleat had wanted me to become a man both off the field and on the field. The Aaron Tighe of a couple of seasons ago had that promise through confidence skill and strength but the Aaron Tighe at the age of 22 was a lad who had been injured for virtually two consecutive seasons and was a high-risk player due to his injury history and was no longer an exciting prospect but a liability to the club. The fact that I was being so aggressive proved that I was up for the challenge but Pleat had to cut a swath through the playing staff numbers and I was on the list. His technique to get rid of players was monstrous to me but it worked and within months he cleared out players and staff left right and centre. He told me that He'd put me on the transfer l ist and would look for opportunities for me, but basically I had to go. The bad man turned nice guy for the rest of our meeting. I wondered how long it would last.

JIM JEFFRIES FALKIRK AND THE END OF THE TRACK

The following day with an arm around my shoulder Pleat explained that Falkirk was looking for a left-sided midfielder and I was to travel up by train the following day. Falkirk at the time was in the Scottish Premier League and was holding their own against the Celtics and Rangers of the Scottish world. After my Leicester experience, I was excited by the prospect of trying out at a new club and looked forward to escaping from the severe all-encompassing Luton pressure. On arrival at Edinburgh train station, I was picked up by a well-mannered gentleman called Jim Jeffries, who I discovered on the drive to Falkirk was the manager of the club. Jim also went on to be the manager of English premier league side Bradford a few seasons back. My impression of him at the time was that he was a true gentleman, with a hard-determined streak, something that you certainly need in football management. My week or so at Falkirk was a success as I found myself playing some excellent football. I felt that my fitnes s levels were good and after training, I'd go out on the cinder track surrounding the Falkirk pitch and work on stamina running. The release of the Luton pressure, my thigh muscles holding up and the fact that I was shining in the training sessions helped boost my confidence. At the end of the trial, Jim Jeffries called me into his office and said He'd offer me a 3-year contract on basically the same money that I had been on at Luton. All he wanted to do was watch me play in a game and He'd come down to Luton to watch me. It was good news. Falkirk was a premier league team and if I did well there, who knows? My injury problems had been forgotten, this was the break I needed. On my return to Luton Pleat immediately involved me in a first-team training session. It was as if he'd had good reports from Jim Jeffries and wanted to have a last look at me. It didn't last long, after about twenty minutes he told me to go and train with the reserves. The man was playing mind games again.

The reserve game that Jim Jeffries came to watch turned out to be one of the worst possible. Luton at the time had dug up the famous plastic pitch and was still preparing the Kenilworth Road grass, hence all reserve games were held at non-league Dunstable's ground, a ground with a rock hard uneven, very little grass surface. Our opponents were Arsenal and I lined up in my least favourite wide left position. My Arsenal opponent was a lively guy by the name of Ray Parlour. The game just never went my way and with the bobbly service, it deteriorated into a touch tackle debacle. After the game, I caught up with Jim Jeffries and he said "Don't worry son, the game just never really went your way" I'll come down and watch you again". It was the last time I'd spoken to Jim. At the same time, Pleat trying hard to off-load me, set me up with a trial in Holland. I can't recall which club, but Holland was of great interest to me from my experience playing there, the football suited me down to the ground and I loved the people. So here I was with a potential move to Falkirk if Jim came back down to watch me and a fantastic opportunity to play in Holland a country that my game would fit well into, however just when I was seeing light fate dealt me a crushing blow.

Whilst training and preparing for the trip to Holland, the inevitable happened, the dreaded thigh muscle problem returned and I was incapacitated. To make matters worse for me the thigh injury was a bad one and going by previous experience would take months rather than weeks to heal properly. Things were looking bleaker than ever. Another Luton midfielder Paul Holsgrove went to Holland in my place and went on to have a successful spell before returning to play for Reading in the UK and Falkirk fell by the wayside with Jim Jeffries obviously picking up another player to fill his wide spot whilst I was injured. It was a truly torrid time for me and the disappointment was immense. To add to my pain at this time Pleat and the club physio Brian (who had only recently arrived) suggested that I get out of football. Having looked at the history of my thigh problems, Pleat remarked "Aaron I think you should look to get another career, like a clerical type job, while you're still young". I wasn't sure if he meant this in sincerity or in a way to offload me but this wasn't as bad as another occasion when I received a phone call from him saying "Aaron why don't you take a holiday in Ireland a couple of weeks, the physio room is overcrowded and I can't afford to have my first team players waiting around while your receiving treatment". Wow, how do you take that? I of course refused and responded with "No I want to get fit I'm not going anywhere". I can say one thing for David at this time; at least he had warned me he was going to make life difficult.

This period of my life was like being on board a runaway train that was running out of track. The train was going to crash, that was for sure, it was inevitable no matter how hard I tried to stop it. Then it happened. In late September of 91, Pleat called me in and made me an offer. The offer was, they would pay up three-quarters of my remaining contract if I left the club immediately. I needed time to think. With my mind racing I tried to weigh up the reality of what was being suggested. The truth was that I couldn't continue to live with the torture and embarrassment of how I was being treated. I had already blown up once and wasn't the kind of person who could just ignore the torment that was being inflicted on me. At the same time I had spent seven years, a third of my life, and all of my short adult life at this football club. The thought of leaving without achieving the full scope of what I set out to do broke my heart. The club had become my home. it was the only life I knew. I was daunted by my future.

Ron Howard had been chief scout at Luton for seven years. He had joined the club at the same time as me. Ron was a wonderful man with a true love of football. In his time at Luton, he had brought to the club players who had been sold for millions. His time had been a true success. In need of advice, he was the first I turned to. To my astonishment, I found that Ron was also under similar pressure, which was a crying shame. Ron, obviously hurt after all the good work he had carried out, didn't tell me what to do but rather cleared the thoughts by bluntly saying "You can take the money and run, or stay and see what happens". The Professional Footballers Union was another source of advice. The guy I spoke to simply said, "If they signed you for three years, then you must have talent, if you decide to go elsewhere you just have to show that talent". These were obvious words of encouragement but I had hidden my concern for my injury problems for fear of alienating myself from any interested parties. The pressure was intense. The fact that I was injured again at this time wasn't helping my case. My pre-season form had been good and if I could have stayed fit I may have been able to hang on in there and impress. The club had definitely abandoned me where fixing my injury was concerned. They simply wanted me out and they made it clear that they were not going to support me. Looking back I may have been able to take all kinds of action against how I was being treated from a Human resources perspective, but unfortunately, good advice at the time was not gained.

> "For now's the time or so they say for stepping out into the night,
> let go, carry on into the night"

> — Aaron Tighe "Into the Night" Copyright© 1991

It was October 1991 and after much soul-searching I decided to take a chance. I'd take the money and search for a new club. The money would give me time to get fit, as I was receiving no physio or help from Luton. Also, I would be away from the dreadful and crushing atmosphere that I was experiencing. It was a chance that had to be taken. A phone call to Ron Howard, Eddie Corcoran (the Dublin scout), and my parents didn't alter my feelings. My family as always gave me their utmost support. In earlier years my Dad would have told me to stay and battle but I believe he understood that I had been battling for a long time and was under enormous strain. Eddie offered me the advice that "the world is your oyster and as one door closes who knows what other doors may open up". Ron offered to try and get me some trials when I was fit, but in his eyes when I spoke to him, I could see that he felt I was making the wrong decision. Looking back I believe Ron knew that once you're on the outside of the professional football club circle, it's not easy to get taken back in, particularly when you have an injury history like mine.

Pleat on the day before I was to finish my professional career, explained the payments that would be made to me, which were spread out over a 6 month period. On inspection, I discovered that they were about 25% short of what was agreed. Pleat argued that this was impossible and forced me to work it out and explain how I had come to my numbers. I also argued that it didn't include the 5000 - pound loyalty fee, which was due at the end of my contract. The club secretary was called in to calculate and after much fuss, discovered that I was in fact short 25% (good job I went to school). The loyalty fee however was not negotiable, as I wasn't completing my contract. By this time I had lost the strength to argue. The mental and emotional strain was beginning to show. These days players have agents to handle negotiations, people who aren't going to be taken advantage of. I wonder what would have happened if I had received a similar service? My career was ending but for Pleat and Co it was just another day's business. The following day I returned to sign forms and whatever formalities were required. The deed had been done, my seven-year roller coaster ride of physical and mental joy and pain was over, just like that, yes, just like that, a simple signing of paperwork and it was all over. It all seemed too easy to be able to leave after years upon years of effort had brought me to this point. Choked, I wandered around the ground saying goodbye to a few office staff, shaking hands with some players and John Moore out on the pitch before picking up my belongings from the changing room and boot room. So many memories and so many ghosts of those who had fallen before me came to mind. It was truly the saddest day of my life. As I left the club, the heavy door closing behind me, and got into my red Vauxhall Astra, the car that had taken me to Leicester and Falkirk, and Ireland for international duty, I felt like a part of me had died. I began to cry uncontrollably and didn't stop until I got home. After dropping my stuff off at home, I headed for the training ground and said goodbye to my mates. I can clearly see the little coach driver Jim Mc Cabe, who had given me and Mark Brearton a stick for not getting on the bus when I first arrived on trial at the age of 14, become emotional when it told him I was leaving. "Why does it happen to the good ones" he said "Go and prove the bastards wrong," he said before shaking my hand. As I returned once again to my car the tears once more began to flow. My thoughts turned to the gypsy that I had spoken to in LA. Little did I know how right she would be. My life was certainly taking a new turn albeit a completely unexpected one. That evening Julie and I sat down to dinner in a daze at what had happened. By coincidence, Julie had finished her job at the airport on exactly the same day. Thinking that we were going to Falkirk, she had given in her notice a few weeks earlier. For the very first time, the two of us were not going to be working the following day. So what's next?

THE CROSSROADS

A local gymnasium became my home for the next couple of weeks of October 1991 as I battled hard to build up my battle-weary thigh muscles. Ron Howard had kindly set up a trial for me at third division (old) Brighton who were looking for a left-sided player and I worked hard to get my fitness levels up. Despite a few calls To Falkirk, Jim Jeffries was unattainable and no calls were returned. I got the message and figured that Jim had been reluctant to pursue me, due to my poor showing against Arsenal and subsequent injury problems, so Brighton was the best bet. Digs were arranged for me on the south coast and I made the 2-and-a-half-hour journey south with a determined mood. During training, I immediately recognised a lower standard of football and was encouraged by my chances to shine. Training went well and certainly, as I had found at Leicester there is a significant gap in standards between the top and lower divisions. An away reserve fixture against Oxford was arranged for the second day of my trial and though I felt that I had impressed in training when the team was read out, I was disappointed to hear that I was to play wide left of four in midfield, a position which relied on service and wasn't a position I had really shone in before. During the game, a mixture of no service, poor football, and a below-par performance I didn't impress anyone. After the game, I felt that I wouldn't have impressed anyone and I was right. Although I joined in training with Brighton for a few more days I learned that I wasn't wanted on the day of the next reserve match, a game against Crystal Palace. After a short training session, the team was read out, and much to my surprise and dismay I wasn't included. Approaching the coach I asked if there had been a mistake as I had been training purposely for the game for about a week "Sorry son" he said, "the Boss saw you play at Oxford and isn't interested". The words hurt deep, one of those sinking feelings that you get in the pit of your stomach. The feeling then gave rise to anger and the major kick in the teeth that I had been given at such a delicate time made me feel like punching the guy for wasting my time. I had worked so hard to get my legs to a level where I could play and was hopeful of at least one more game. Why bother keeping me down their training if I wasn't wanted? After picking up my stuff from my digs I set out on the long drive home to Luton. I can remember clearly a radio DJ announcing that Freddie Mercury the lead singer of Queen had died of aids that day. It was a sad long drive home.

On my return to Luton and with the Christmas of 1991 approaching, I continued my daily training regime of gym and ball work in the local park, whilst trying to figure out what the hell I was going to do. These were dark days in my life, a cloud had descended and all I could think of was working hard to get fit and hoping for an opportunity to arise. I was no longer employed, had a woeful history of a recurring injury that seemed to be getting worse with each new tear and had missed the boat with Holland, Falkirk, and Brighton. I can recall looking to the heavens one day at the park where I was training and asking for help, serious times! My state of mind is clearly etched out in some songs that I wrote at the time.

Aaron Tighe

Eyes That See No Better Days

Two weeks of hell, a lonely see strand
A riptide pulls at my body and soul
Justice today is my latest demand
The waves they crash then take control
Believe me now for tonight I am strong
First light of morning will seize the day
Too late now what's done is done
In mornings whispers you hear me pray

Run tonight through these city streets
Reach out beyond the silent gaze
Of eyes that see no better days
Of eyes that see no better days

Tonight I am sorrow tonight I am greed
Immune to the danger that happiness brings
Faith in your teachings I will always believe
Blessings or curse are not what they seem
The words are spoken a strangers tongue
The news it spins then flies away
The winds of change may prove me wrong
But who are you now to stand in my way

Run tonight through these city streets
Reach out beyond the silent gaze
Of eyes that see no better days
Of eyes that see no better days

Disguise

it's like running in the darkness
Being blinded by the light
it's like seeing the pain of another mans life
In the orange glow of a streetlamp
In the shadows cast by the moon
I've touched the hand of forgiveness
Seen that love is true

Oh my love be strong, Oh my love carry on
I have searched and found shelter in your eyes
You say that hurt is a blessing in disguise

Does surrender lead to grief
Tell me now is it brave to fall
Doubt can sometimes smother belief
Or am I just a fool
Walk with me around the world
We'll watch the dawn of time
Race the wind and chase the moon
Reach up and touch the sky

I always long to see her though we're never apart
I would weep like the smallest child
If ever she were to break my heart.

Oh my love be strong, Oh my love carry on.
I have searched and found shelter in your eyes
You say that hurt is a blessing in disguise

Literally on the afternoon that I had gazed to the cloudy grey
heavens and asked for help an amazing thing happened in the
Gym. Robin Wainwright, a Gym staff member, who looked like

he'd stepped directly out of a seventies rock band with his long scraggly hair, approached me and we started talking about football. Lo and behold as we talked I discovered that I had played for Luton in Robin's testimonial match a few seasons back at non-league Wealdstone. That particular game was a memorable one for me because of some of the quality players on show, people like Stuart Pearce the England International who was playing for Wealdstone and Luton's first team of Donaghy, Foster, Hill, Stein, Grimes etc, plus me and one or two other fringe players. As we talked I informed Robin of my recent departure from Luton and the fact that I was just trying to stay fit. "Hey why don't you come down to Hitchin Town to keep fit?" asked Robin. Hitchin were a local non-league side situated 20 minutes or so outside of Luton. "Rob Johnson is coming down and we've got Stuart Brown and Darren Thompson" Robin continued. Rob Johnson had been a Luton stalwart for all of his career and a terrific bloke. He had only recently retired from pro football. Stuart and Darren were ex-apprentices who had recently been released by the club. "You'll enjoy it, it's a good bunch of lads", exclaimed Robin.

Was it simply coincidence or fate meeting Robin Wainwright? Whatever it was it changed my life and that's for sure. I was truly at a crossroads and didn't know where to turn at the time of meeting Robin but from that moment on my life had a path again. Although initially it was only a way to keep fit, things changed when I scored on my debut for them in a local Derby against rivals Stevenage. By the arrival of the New Year the Manager and owner Andy Melvin had offered me, along with a few other ex-Luton lads, work in an accounts department, which supplemented the Hitchin expenses that were being paid out. Although a turn away from professional football, my options were limited and choices had to be made to keep an income coming in. Luckily I was, as I mentioned before, someone who carried on with education during my football years, which stood me in good stead for a career outside of football. No interest had been shown from the transfer list whilst still at Luton and no more interest had been shown from professional clubs as an x pro. Over a number of months, I came to a realization that in truth I was a player with a long history of recurring injuries, which were getting worse and I was 22 years old and no longer a bright starlet that a club could afford to carry. The dream that I had cherished when I was a kid was no longer shining bright for me, football was no longer something I enjoyed, in fact, it hadn't been for years if I'm truthful. The mental and physical battering over the years had brought home a realisation that maybe the dizzy heights weren't to be my fate and perhaps my professional life lay outside of the football inner circle. don't get me wrong, I have as I said at the beginning and have hopefully mentioned had fantastic times in football. However, I was someone who deep inside throughout my life had felt that winning was the only option! My blighted injury-ravaged experiences leading up to this point had been nothing short of traumatic, a feeling that was all too consuming. These experiences over particularly the latter years had continually thwarted my progress. I couldn't keep on losing. I couldn't keep on experiencing that heartbreak. I had to change and change I did.

I remained with Hitchin Town for two seasons, unfortunately playing only a handful of games each season due to my beleaguered thigh problems, but the period, apart from my injuries, was a good one and some close friendships with people like Ken Gillard, Captain Mark Burke and their wonderful wives Lorraine and Marion were established. The pressure that had weighed me down like a tonne of bricks on my shoulders lifted almost immediately during my first Hitchin Town training session. Enjoyment in football had been found again and I learned that, incredible as it seemed, there was life outside of professional football. The team went on to have two successful FA Cup runs featured on Match of the Day during my time although I was injured for all of the games. It was a good club and attracted some excellent players like former Spurs and Wales defender Paul Price, Tottenham and

Aaron Tighe

Chelsea star Micky Hazard, a player who had been a hero of mine and Luton and England's own Ricky Hill. Fellow Luton midfielder and good friend Ian Scott also joined the club along with ex-Luton and close friend Ken Gillard, which made it like playing for Luton, a home from home. On the work front, the experience of working in an accounts department gave me an excellent grounding for future endeavours in the world of sales and Management, a profession that would prove to be an outstanding success for me and not too unlike the competitive arena of professional football. On the home front, Julie and I had the perfect wedding on September 3rd, 1993 at St Joseph's church Luton, a day that is a precious memory and thank God is wonderfully captured on video. What did people do before video cameras? It was great to see some of my old pals at the wedding, Mickser Obrien, Ken Gillard, Scotty, Reecy, Mal Donaghy, Fazza, Tommo, and Browny amongst others.

And so it was that my football-playing career drew to a close on a late wintry November night in 1994. Earlier during the summer break we decided to employ the expertise of the excellent surgeon 'Dr Dorrell' to find a solution to my thigh problems. As this was a private medical function, records were required on the injury. We discovered somewhat disappointingly that Luton Town had lost all of my medical records and couldn't help with any of the history of my lengthy treatments to date. This was very unusual and perhaps if looked upon with suspicion I could have pursued it further, but certainly any actions against the club weren't the intention. The operation on my left thigh followed anyway when we found a way around the medical records problem and a full pre-season was duly completed without hitch with the usual regime of building up my thigh muscles for a two to 3 month period. Dr Dorrell pointed out post-operation that although he had removed wedges of scar tissue from my left thigh there was no guarantee of a recovery due to the fact that by operating more scar tissue would be created. True to form and as if to prove the Doctor right the leg broke down in the first game of the season whilst sprinting for a ball midway through the second half. All the hard work after the operation seemed wasted. We still carried on with building up the leg again, however after a few more breakdowns over a period of 6 months, some happening embarrassingly after coming on as a substitute; I decided to call it a day. It had been seven years since the first thigh injury occurred and despite best efforts from myself, specialist physios, surgeons, and doctors I figured that too much damage had been done. As I looked up at the stars after yet another breakdown on the Hitchin football pitch, I felt that the flame that had once shone so bright was flickering out. Playing football was not the way forward for me and a new career had to be sought from the 'Green' of Banbury to the green grass of Hitchin, a long up and down journey had been traveled over the course of my football years and my life was rich from the experience. I had succeeded in my amazing "shoot for the moon" dream of becoming a professional footballer with international status and that was, and is something I will treasure forever. Everyone's journey along that path must come to an end at some stage and my time just happened a little sooner than I expected. Although I never quite reached the heights that I sought so hard to achieve, even though at times they were agonisingly within touching distance, boy what a go I gave it, I was a Player for a time! And will never forget it.

THE END

AND FINALLY

I have mentioned many names throughout my story and it is incredible to look at the varied journeys that we have taken during our young adult lives. Some made it big, some made it small, and many were forced to venture into a life outside of football. Here's what happened to a few of the young professionals that I grew up with at Luton and provides an insight into how tough it is to make it as a pro footballer, get to the top, and then stay there for a long period.

Ricky Macca Mc Evoy (the hugely talented youth and under 21 international) - Football Career in Irish football after a number of 1st team appearances.

Marcus Tuite (scored a winner for Ireland against Brazil during a youth World Cup and wouldn't ever let us forget it!) - returned to Dublin at 18, a career outside of football.

Gary Cobby Cobb (Quoted by Manager Ray Harford as the best crosser of a ball at the club, a top 6 English club at the time)— Non-league career after a number of first-team appearances.

David Oldfield (pace, athleticism, and dedication) - Successful pro career with Man City, Leicester, Stoke, and Luton amongst others.

Aaron Tighe

Jason Reecy Reece (the Welsh international dynamo and the real "Bizzy") - Pro career with Luton, Portsmouth and Exeter.

Mick Mickser Obrien (I ish youth international and the most talented schoolboy David Pleat had ever seen) - broken leg complications ended his career before it got started.

Ian Scotty Scott (In the first team squad at 16 a classy player) - non-league career with Hitchin Town.

Richard Harvey (a man amongst boys England schoolboy and youth) - Pro career with Luton until retired mid-twenties through injury.

Ken Gilly Gillard (Youth Irish international) Short career with Luton, Ireland youth and Northampton before a Knee injury retired him in his early twenties.

Alan Sully O'Sullivan (Irish schoolboy international). Left Luton at the end of his initial contract, a career outside of football.

Neil Poutchy Poutch (Irish schoolboy, youth and under 21 international) - Made a couple of first-team appearances before being released by Jim Ryan. Neil went home to Ireland. Career outside of football.

Darren Salts Big Man Salton (Scottish youth international and regular first-team player at 18) - had a shocking car crash that very nearly cost him his life and finished his playing career.

Paul Telf Telfer (One of the fittest and most dedicated footballers I met). Has had a very successful career with Scotland, Luton, Coventry Celtic, and Southampton.

Kingsley Kings Black (A winger who would leave defenders on their backside). Successful pro career with Luton, Northern I reland, Nottingham Forest, and Grimsby.

Marvin Marv Johnson (Excellent career with Luton eventually captaining the club).

Sean Fazza Farrell (Plenty of 1st team appearances before having a good career in the lower divisions). I think he was wasted and should have been the next George Michael.

Mark Pembo Pembridge (Huge career with Luton, Wales, Sheffield Wednesday, Benfica, Everton and Fulham).

Ceri Chad Hughes (Pro career with Luton and Wimbledon amongst others).

Matthew Mattie Jackson (After a few Premier League first-team appearances at Luton was picked up by Everton)

John Hartson (Huge career with Arsenal, West Ham, Celtic)

Aaron Tighe now resides in Perth Western Australia with Julie and children Sean and Megan. Aaron forged a highly successful career in the world of telecommunications in Senior Management roles in the UK and for a leading Australian Telecommunications company and has remained involved in the beautiful game as a youth coach assisting young players by passing on his skills, experience, and knowledge to thousands of young players, some who have gone on to have successful careers in professional football via Luton Town youth and the Tighe Soccer Academy in Perth www.tighesoccer.biz

"Time is a servant to wisdom"

— Aaron Tighe "The shock" Copyright© 1991

JOBS - ROSTER

MARVIN JOHNSON — A. DIBBLE ①, S. FOSTER ②
IAN SCOTT — M. HARFORD ④ P. NICHOLAS ⑤
RICHARD HARVEY — B. STEIN ⑥ G. PARKER ⑦
DUNCAN BERRY — E. NWAJIOBI ⑧ P. ELLIOTT ⑨
DAVID OLDFIELD — R. JOHNSON ⑩ M. DONAGHY ⑫
AARON TIGHE — R. HILL ⑭ A. GRIMES ⑮
JOHN KENNEDY — L. SEALEY ⑯ D. PREECE ⑱
PAUL LEWIS — W. TURNER ⑲ M. THOMAS ⑳
MATTHEW BOWDEN — R. DANIEL ㉑ S. NORTH ㉒
SEAN FARRELL — M. NORTH ㉓ T. BREACKER ㉕
NEIL POUCH — M. STEIN ㉖ M. TUITE ㉔
GARY COBB — STAFF

WEEK 15ᵀᴴ JULY — 21ˢᵗ JULY

EQUIPMENT: Pumping of Balls, Bibs, Cones etc, — From Ground — into Shed —
            onto Pitches. — R. HARVEY, A. TIGHE.

CLEANING OF DRESSING ROOM   A: J. KENNEDY
                            B: M. JOHNSON
                            C: S. FARRELL

BATH & SHOWER AREA: P. LEWIS

LUNCH & KITCHEN AREA: CLEANING PLATES, CUPS ETC, — I. SCOTT, N. POUCH

SOCCER BOOTS: TO BE TIED, PUT AWAY IN SKIPS ETC. — D. BERRY, M. BOWDEN

STAFF AREA: G. COBB

Aaron Tighe

This isn't the glamorous story of a football superstar and legend that will have left fingerprints on the memories of football fans the world over. It is however a familiar story, one that is recognised by everyone, who as a kid, lost themselves in a beautiful football world, a world of camaraderie with friends and competitors, a world of running, passing, tackling, dribbling, shooting and dreaming just for that moment in time, that anything was possible.

Aaron's story takes you through his early football endeavours with his school friends and family in the local streets and parks of England, his recognition as an outstanding International schoolboy football talent in Ireland, and subsequent trials with top-flight English clubs Chelsea and Luton Town, eventuating in a seven-year professional and International career at the heights of English football.

For anyone who seeks an insight into the transition from schoolboy footballer to professional footballer, the twists and turns and highs and lows of a young footballers life, Aaron's story will show you 'what it takes.'